The Psychology of High Abilities

Also by Michael J. A. Howe

Understanding School Learning
Learning in Infants and Young Children
Adult Learning
Learning from Television
Introduction to Human Memory
A Teachers' Guide to the Psychology of Learning
Television and Children
The Psychology of Human Learning
Introduction to the Psychology of Memory
Fragments of Genius: the Strange Feats of Idiots Savants
Encouraging the Development of Exceptional Skills and Talents
Sense and Nonsense about Hothouse Children
Give Your Child a Better Start (*with Harriet Griffey*)
Principles of Human Abilities and Learning
IQ in Question: The Truth about Intelligence

The Psychology of High Abilities

Michael J. A. Howe

MACMILLAN

First published 1999 by
MACMILLAN PRESS LTD
Houndmills, Basingstoke, Hampshire RG21 6XS
and London
Companies and representatives throughout the world

ISBN 0–333–75096–9 hardcover
ISBN 0–333–75097–7 paperback

A catalogue record for this book is available from the British Library.

This book is printed on paper suitable for recycling and made from fully managed and sustained forest sources.

10 9 8 7 6 5 4 3 2 1
08 07 06 05 04 03 02 01 00 99

Editing and origination by
Aardvark Editorial, Mendham, Suffolk

Printed in Hong Kong

Contents

Preface

High abilities are a vital human resource, and the aim of *The Psychology of High Abilities* is to explain how, when and why people acquire them, and illuminate ways of making it possible for larger numbers of young people to extend their capabilities. It was originally intended that *The Psychology of High Abilities* would be a shorter and more up-to-date version of an earlier book, *The Origins of Exceptional Abilities*, which was first published in 1990. However, it soon became apparent that the changes would need to be far more substantial than I had anticipated, and less than half of *The Psychology of High Abilities* is directly based on the earlier book.

Because high abilities are so valuable, there is much to be gained from striving to understand their causes. It is not always easy to know for certain why one individual rather than another has gained impressive capabilities. Explaining that can be so difficult, and there is always a temptation to assume that the origins of exceptional abilities are a complete mystery. There is also a tendency for people to assume that special genes or special innate gifts must be at the root of unusual capabilities, without even stopping to establish whether or not there is a scientific justification for that assumption. Simply because they cannot think of alternative explanations, some people leap to the conclusion that innate talents must be the cause. In reality, as soon as one seriously looks for them, a substantial number of other influences that contribute to individual variability in human abilities become evident.

We cannot manufacture geniuses, but we can take steps that substantially increase the likelihood of young people acquiring high degrees of competence in various fields of expertise, and enjoying lives that are productive and successful as well as fulfilling. And although our knowledge of the causes of the most exceptional abilities is certainly incomplete, we do know sufficient to make it possible to design and implement educational policies that could lead to substantial increase in the proportion of young people who master the difficult skills that society rightly values.

My thanks to the numerous individuals who have helped to make this book possible. They include John Sloboda, Jane Davidson, Steve Ceci, John Radford, Joan Freeman and Anders Ericsson, as well as a number of other friends and colleagues. At Macmillans, Frances Arnold has been especially helpful and encouraging. Thanks also to Sylvia, for her constant support.

Chapter 1

Some influences on abilities

High abilities are, to say the least, extremely valuable. They are valuable to the individual who gains them, because they magnify any person's chances of enjoying an adulthood that is fruitful, constructive, and successful. The individual who acquires special expertise may or may not become capable of the highest creative accomplishments, but many kinds of high abilities extend their possessors' capacities to enjoy life and experience the sense of fulfilment that productive efforts can help to bring about.

High abilities can also be valuable to the broader society their owner inhabits. Expertise gets things done. Acquired competence helps make enterprises run smoothly and efficiently. An exceptionally capable individual's really outstanding accomplishments can inspire other people. The most impressive achievements of all may create revolutions that transform the daily experiences and the long-term outlooks of numerous men and women.

What is meant by the word 'ability'? It has been defined in various ways by different people. For our purposes, however, a very precise definition would be restrictive and counterproductive. When I introduce the word I have in mind broadly the same band of meanings that are elicited by its synonyms, such as 'capability', 'attainment', 'competence', 'acquired capacity' or 'accomplishment'.

Broadly speaking, abilities are made up from varying combinations of the things that a person becomes able to do ('skills') and the useful information that the person has gained ('knowledge'). Human abilities are essentially acquired, as a consequence of deliberate or incidental learning. Yet they may be affected by, or depend upon, innate biological qualities of the person.

The main aim of this book is to explore the circumstances that give rise to high abilities. How and why do certain people become experts? What causes particular individuals to be unusually capable? What are some of the causes of genius? How does being a child prodigy affect someone's chances of having an especially productive adult career?

In this chapter I begin by looking at three of the most common responses that are supplied when ordinary people are confronted with these questions. These are

1. it is a matter of training and hard work;
2. it all depends upon having a good early start;
3. high abilities are made possible by innate gifts and talents.

All of these responses are ones that we shall return to in later chapters, but in the present one a start will be made by introducing some of the research that has supplied relevant evidence and cast light on the matter. In the case of the first two responses ('training and hard work' and 'an early start') we shall quickly discover that while they are partial and incomplete answers they do each contain a large element of truth. In considering the third answer ('innate talents') I shall arrive at a more critical conclusion, and the present chapter's brief discussion of some of the issues will be expanded upon in Chapter 7.

Training and hard work

At school, there are always a few pupils who stay at the top of the class and flourish in examinations but are rumoured to do so without ever studying at all. These are the students who tend to be admired most by others. Unlike the often-despised class-room swots, who are perceived as succeeding by drudgery and unglamorous hard work, those who appear to be effortlessly successful are much esteemed: their apparently natural brilliance is regarded as an admirable and greatly envied quality.

Whether or not such pupils actually exist within the higher reaches of most schools, there is no doubt that there are many young people who strive to ensure that any efforts they make to do well at school are carefully hidden from their classmates. Appearing studious is hardly cool. Success itself is desirable and to be envied, but because it is only seen as estimable when it is effortless, a great deal of energy goes into concealing studying activities from other students.

These studiers-in-secret often do well at examinations, partly because, unlike many of their peers, they have cottoned on to the fact that succeeding at academic studies does require making an effort. Although widely believed to be true, the idea that there are some fortunate individuals who gain unusual degrees of expertise without any effort at all is largely false. Doing well at most areas of competence does require hard work. Impressive capabilities are only gained as a consequence of prolonged training and experience. To become highly accomplished in any area of skill or field of knowledge necessitates extended periods of learning.

Of course, the particular form of the necessary learning experiences depends upon the kind of capability that is being acquired. For example, much of the musical training that a person needs to undertake in order to become a competent performer takes the form of practising at the instrument. Central to the training needed by a mathematician is frequent exposure to mathematical problems. But whatever the precise nature of the training activities, the sheer amount of studying has to be substantial, and in most cases it must involve deliberate and effortful studying. And the training activities also have to be appropriate ones, designed to extent the person's capabilities. So just messing around with a guitar does not make a person into a great performer, and a weekly round of golf or game of tennis does not necessarily produce huge improvements in an amateur player's skills.

Research investigating the progress of young instrumental musicians has drawn attention to necessity for regular and frequent practising in order for a student to become a competent performer. By the time they reach the standard of a competent amateur player, young musicians will have devoted something in the region of three thousands hours to practising at their instrument (Sloboda *et al.*, 1996). That is a lot of time. Of course, a few players manage to get by with considerably less, but in our research, which examined the musical development of a number of young people, we uncovered no cases at all of individuals who had made good progress without doing substantial amounts of practising.

That is not to say that practising is the only cause of musical excellence, or that the sheer amount of practice is all-important. Nevertheless, we did discover that the cumulative time that a young person had spent practising was a good predictor of the extent to which progress had been made towards becoming an expert instrumentalist. Indeed, among all the measures we had available, assessments of the amount of practising an individual had undertaken turned out to be the best single predictors of that person's success.

That is especially impressive in view of the fact that our assessments of time spent practising were somewhat rough and ready ones. They suffered from various limitations. For example, the measures of amount of time devoted to practising were retrospective. They often depended on young musicians' hazy recollections about the time they spent practising up to ten years earlier. Clearly, the accuracy of information collected retrospectively will not always be high. Also, the measures of practising took no account of the appropriateness of the practising activities that were being engaged in. Presumably, this would have varied appreciably, and would have depended upon factors such as the differing astuteness of particular teachers. Finally, the assessments of practising took no account of the care and attentiveness that were going into the activity. Presumably, there would have been times when a student was concentrating hard, diligently determined to get things right and make progress, and other times when a learner was feeling tired or bored and merely going through the motions of practising while daydreaming about tonight's date or tomorrow's football match. In the somewhat crude assessments we were able to make, these varying circumstances were simply lumped together.

The fact that assessments of practising were good predictors of success despite suffering from the disadvantages of all three of these limitations reinforces the conclusion that practice is indeed important. It seems very likely that when it becomes possible to obtain more accurate and more detailed assessments of practising over long periods of time than the ones currently available, relationships between measures of performance and cumulative measures of practising will be seen to be even more substantial than the ones we have observed up until now.

However, to be effective in yielding high levels of expertise, practising and study activities do need to be systematic, deliberate, and extended (Ericsson and Charness, 1994). The amateur tennis player who is aware of the limitations of his backhand shots may improve his performance a little by making an effort to practise backhands in next week's game. But for the professional player that kind of practising would be seen as not remotely sufficient. The professional will be more likely to set up a practice session in which the particular shot that is inadequate can be repeatedly practised, hundreds or even thousands of times. Similarly, an aspiring musical performer may practise for several hours each day. Rather than just playing pieces that are enjoyable, the would-be professional player will devote time to repeated scales and make repetitive attempts to master particular passages that cause difficulty.

In many areas of expertise, the highest levels of mastery are only attained after deliberate training that extends over thousands of hours. A young professional musician will typically have devoted around ten thousand hours to practice and training. A similar amount of time will be needed for the training of a chess master. Comparable periods of training are also necessary in other areas of expertise, ranging from athletics to architecture, mathematics and medicine, and from football to the physical sciences (Charness *et al.*, 1996; Ericsson, 1996; Glaser, 1996; Patel *et al.*, 1996; Starkes *et al.*, 1996). The hard work that goes into frequent and regular periods of deliberate training may not be *sufficient* to ensure the highest levels of expertise and mastery, but it is undoubtedly a *necessary* condition.

A good start

There have been people who have made great achievements despite suffering early deprivation or other childhood circumstances that have given them a poor start in life. The great railway engineer George Stephenson became a genius despite the fact that he never went to school at all, and Michael Faraday became a brilliant scientist although he had to leave school at thirteen. So having a good start is not an indispensable precursor of a life of high achievement.

All the same, a good start is undoubtedly helpful, and the vast majority of individuals whose adult lives have been unusually creative or productive, or who have been unusually capable within various fields of expertise, have been people whose early years have been stimulating ones, characterized by plenty of opportunities to learn, and plenty of guidance and encouragement, often given by one or both parents. I expand on the parents' role in encouraging early learning in Chapter 2. There I describe, for example, some research findings demonstrating that young people differ enormously of their actual experiences of language. Such experiences have large effects on children's linguistic competence. Children benefit very considerably from having lots of opportunities to listen to language messages that are specifically directed towards them. They also benefit from having opportunities to practise at using language to express their own thoughts.

It is not at all hard to understand why having a good start increases the likelihood of a young person eventually becoming an especially capable adult. Consider, for example, the advantage of gaining above-average language skills at an early age. Acquiring language affects a child's capacities as a thinker in some fundamental ways. Language also makes possible an explosive growth in a child's capacity to retain information in memory. That in turn opens up the possibility of undertaking cognitive activities such as planning, reasoning and making choices and judgements, and anticipating the future, which are literally inconceivable in a species that lacks language. In sum, acquiring language brings about a complete transformation in what a child is capable of. As a result, those children who gain the advantages that are brought by the early acquisition of language skills will have their capacity to learn from their experiences magnified considerably.

Of course, almost all children do eventually gain language, even when their early circumstances are unfavourable. Unfortunately, however, young people whose early language experiences are relatively impoverished, perhaps because little language is directed towards the child by the parents or other adults, will suffer from the disadvantages of acquiring language later than those children who receive plenty of help and encouragement. Also, the mastery of language by children whose progress is slower is likely to remain incomplete. To do well at school it is necessary to have good language skills rather than merely possessing rudimentary ones, and the benefits of above-average early progress tend to be maintained.

One particular benefit for a young child of having a good command of one's own language is that this makes it easier for a child to learn to read. There are various reasons for this, one being that learning reading skills is facilitated when the learner is able to make fine discriminations between similar sounds. Certainly, children who have been encouraged to gain the habit of listening carefully to what people say will have a marked advantage here. Such a habit (and the listening skills that it promotes) is especially likely to be acquired by children whose parents regularly read to them. Hence, through the activity of reading to children, those parents who are able to devote time and attention to guiding their children and giving them help and opportunities aimed at helping them to learn, can bring real benefits to their sons and daughters.

Why is reading so important, and why is it beneficial for a child to have a good early start? A key function of reading is to make the learner considerably more autonomous and independent than would otherwise be possible. The young reader is less dependent upon adults, reading being a way in which the individual can make progress alone, extending knowledge, gaining information, and learning about the world and its possibilities from books and stories. Reading breaks through the constraints of daily life and the limitations of the home environment, and gives the young reader access to a much wider and more varied world.

Of course, learning to read early is not all-important. Unless children clearly want to learn to read earlier than usual, and are likely to take advantage of the possible benefits of early reading, it may bring few if any real benefits. Even so, the child who is encouraged to gain good language skills and is frequently read to will still have advantages. That is because such children, when they do begin to learn to read (typically at school) are likely to have far fewer problems with learning to read than children whose early home backgrounds have not provided these experiences. The main reason for that is that the ease of learning to read, which is not an easy accomplishment, depends considerably on the extent to which the child has already acquired a variety of basic language skills that reading depends upon. So the child whose family experiences have encouraged the healthy growth of language skills, and in particular the ones that are extended by the kinds of listening experiences a child gains from being read to, will be at an advantage whenever, whether sooner or later, the child is taught reading as such.

Of course, there are numerous different ways in which parents and others can act in order to help give children a better start in life. 'Guiding' is a better word than 'teaching' to indicate the kinds of activities that are most effective for helping young children. As guides, sensitive parents help their children to make sense of the world. For instance, they may draw a child's attention to events that are important, or point out objects that are especially significant to the growing child.

These guiding activities need to be informal if they are to be effective. They may often be provided in the context of game or play situations. Moreover, parents have to be careful to avoid acting in ways that can put a child off learning. For example, a parent has to be conscious of the fact that young children's attention spans may be very short, and prepared to defer an activity just as soon as the child's attention or enthusiasm shows signs of wavering. Otherwise, a situation can arise in which, from the child's point of view, pressure is being placed on a young person to stay with an activity that only the parent is keen to persist at.

It is equally important to avoid situations in which the child is made to feel that there is any kind of criticism involved, or expression of disappointment, or in which a parent is perceived as being too anxious for the child to do well. Children do enjoy praise and encouragement, but too much emphasis upon doing well, or too much attention to praising children at the times they are most obviously successful, can have the effect of communicating the idea that success is all-important. If only because of the experiences of pressure that are likely to result from this, young children are most likely to make good progress when they do not have to deal with feelings relating to doing well, or competing. It is far better for the parents to provide situations in which young children are engaging in activities simply because they enjoy them, especially if those activities just happen to be ones that help young learners to gain knowledge or skill that will extend their mental powers.

With the youngest children, and especially in the first year of life, it is important for parents to appreciate that during much of their child's waking time the child will not be in the relaxed-but-alert state of mind that is most conducive to learning. Often a child will be too hungry or too tired or fractious or over-excited, or too irritated, to show much interest in the toy that the mother would like her to enjoy or to participate in the game that the father is anxious to share. Sensitive parents learn how to spot when the time is ripe to engage in play activities that help a child to learn, and reign back their enthusiasm on other occasions.

So, broadly speaking, whenever a child gives signs of not enjoying an activity, or becoming bored, or tired, or anxious, or overly excited, it is best for parents to retreat. So far as young children are concerned, the circumstances in which valuable learning is most likely to take place are ones in which the interaction between parent and child is informal, laid-back and playful, and in which both parties can be free and spontaneous in their behaviour. Of course, it is not always easy for a parent to arrange that. It takes powers of sensitivity and a well-developed capacity to see things from a child's point of view. Clearly, being a conscientious guide demands considerable care and patience, as well as sensitivity. These qualities are not innate: parents have to learn for themselves how to be effective guides for their own sons and daughters.

Formal teaching skills are less necessary. The job of the parent is less one of instilling knowledge than of giving the child opportunities to have experiences that will give rise to learning. Fortunately, in doing this parents have the big advantage of having had time to get to know their own children as individuals. Professional teachers are less advantaged in this respect: a classroom teacher may be responsible for educating thirty or more young children but have fewer opportunities to learn about each child's personal interests and idiosyncrasies.

The kinds of parental activities that are effective sometimes involve taking steps to encourage learning at a younger age than may ostensibly seem appropriate. Take language for example. Most children do not utter their first word until around the end of year one, so it might appear that there is little point in a parent becoming concerned about encouraging language development until then. In fact, however, that conclusion would be mistaken, because a child's capacity to speak builds upon and depends upon skills that are gained long before the earliest words are actually uttered. Active speech is far from being the beginning of language: it is the end-product of a considerable amount of language learning. Signs that a baby is beginning to *understand* language may be present as early as the fourth month.

A baby who is regularly talked to from an early age will gain essential communication skills that language builds upon. Such a child will become familiar with the sounds that language uses. She will also learn how to produce those sounds, and discover that various sounds can represent objects and experiences. In addition, the child will learn from the parents to engage in a kind of activity that is basic to all languages, the capacity to take turns at attending to another person and responding to them. This turn-taking is basic to a particularly crucial aspect of language communication, its conversational element. The child who is encouraged to engage in turn-taking games and activities such as 'pat-a-cake' will learn a great deal about how people communicate with one another, through conversation-like activities.

In short, the good early start that caring parents can provide brings real advantages. As we have seen, that is even true in the case of a universal human capacity such as language, which our brains are innately prepared for, and despite the fact that most children will acquire langauge sooner or later, even if their parents do not frequently talk to them.

However, it is also important to realize that having a good early start cannot guarantee that a child will have an especially fruitful adult life. And it is equally true that plenty of individuals who have *not* enjoyed a particularly stimulating or happy childhood have nevertheless enjoyed highly creative lives. All the same, it is correct to say that, other things being equal, having a good early start gives a child real advantages.

Innate gifts and talents

Many people are totally convinced that in order for a person to be especially successful in various fields of accomplishment it is essential for that individual to have been born possessing special qualities. According to that viewpoint, only a child who has an innate gift for music can aspire to becoming an exceptional musician. The same principle is believed to apply in various other areas of special expertise, ranging from sporting activities to the arts.

Whether or not innate talents are crucial, or even exist at all, is a matter of controversy. In Chapter 7, I discuss some of the arguments and introduce some of the research findings that can help to settle the issue. However, in most of the other chapters little or no attention will be given to innate talents as a possible cause of high abilities.

That may seem an eccentric way to proceed. Many teachers and others would claim that the evidence pointing to the importance of innate gifts and talents is compelling. Numerous experienced musicians, for instance, insist that only a child with an inborn gift for music can expect to do well, and that identifying and nurturing innate potentials are crucial activities in the promotion of musical excellence. These experts would think it absurd to investigate high abilities and their causes without taking innate talents into account.

Ostensibly, the evidence that innate talents exist is quite impressive. It is only necessary to compare a couple of five-year-olds' first responses to musical instruction to see that even by that age, even though neither child has yet received any formal musical training, two children can be remarkably different in their capabilities. One child seems to take to music enthusiastically, and makes steady progress from the beginning, while the other child struggles to learn, with little or no success. Surely, it appears, differences in competence that are so substantial, and appear so early in life, must be innate. What alternative causes could there possibly be?

In the face of the strongly held beliefs about innate gifts and talents it is tempting to concede that they are crucial. However, matters of enormous practical importance revolve around the question of their existence, and so the issue demands more careful investigation. A particularly important reason why it is essential to arrive at the truth is that numerous young people are discriminated against on the basis of adults' assumptions that they are devoid of talents that are necessary for success. For example, in various selection processes, in which a minority of applicants are chosen to receive special training that is in short supply (usually because is too expensive to provide for every child), the teachers or other adults who engage in the activity of choosing a small number of children generally do so on the basis of their conviction that talent is crucial. The children thus selected are believed to be ones who, unlike the others, are innately gifted and are therefore capable of gaining maximum advantage from the training they are given.

Since in the absence of special training opportunities a child's likelihood of success will be greatly reduced, perhaps to zero, the experience of being selected can make a huge difference to the course of a child's future life. For the many who fail to be chosen, a door is effectively closed in their faces. These children are barred from making progress by being denied vital learning opportunities. So it is vital to ensure that the grounds for their being barred – their assumed lack of innate talent – really are genuine ones. Unless this can be confirmed, it is impossible to refute the suggestion that numerous young people are being arbitrarily and unfairly denied access to facilities and opportunities that could enable them to do well.

The detailed arguments and evidence for and against the talent account will have to wait until Chapter 7. For the present, here are some findings which point to the necessity to look more closely at certain kinds of evidence that at first appear to provide strong confirmation of the existence of innate gifts. On closer examination it can be seen that quite different explanations are more convincing.

The first kind of evidence that initially seems to point to innate causes of the differing skills of individuals comes from Africa. There are certain very marked differences between European and African infants in the rate at which movement-based abilities develop. For example, it is known that many African infants gain skills such as sitting and walking appreciably earlier than infants in Europe and America do. These differences have been observed in a number of cross-cultural research studies. They have been seen as demonstrating that human variability in patterns of competence must be innately determined, by factors that reflect individuals' varying racial origins.

Second, in a psychological investigation it was discovered that one young man was able to remember lists of up to 80 random digits. After one presentation of a list he could recall the whole sequence without making any errors at all. It has long been assumed that people's natural ability to retain items in memory is unchangeable, and there is firm evidence that the maximum list length that most people can recall is around eight or nine items. So there appears to be no way of avoiding the conclusion that this particular young man, who successfully recalled lists about ten times as long as those that the average person could remember, must have possessed a fundamentally exceptional capacity to remember. It is hard to think of any other explanation for someone being able to recall ten times as much information as other people could.

Third, in another study, which involved a kind of video game in which coloured objects moved around a screen, volunteers tried to identify various kinds of briefly presented visual stimuli. The design of the study included certain visual masking events which had the effect of making the stimuli very hard to perceive. But the investigators found that one particular individual could always identify all the items with perfect accuracy, even under difficult conditions. His expertise contrasted very sharply with that of the other participants: most of them could only identify the items correctly if they were presented for two or three times as long as this person required. So once more, it would appear that the individual, like the young man in the previous example, must have possessed certain mental abilities that were inherently superior to those of ordinary people.

Finally, in yet another investigation, a five-year-old child was observed to swim and dive with tremendous skill, and to operate with impressive mastery a canoe that was known to be extremely hard for most adults to control. The feats performed by this particular child were so immensely superior to anything that children of the same age are normally able to achieve that, once again, the conclusion that special inherent capabilities must have been present appears to be inescapable.

Each of these three instances presents us with a situation that seems to point quite unambiguously to the existence of some special inborn gift or inherent capability that ordinary individuals lack. If it could be shown that, despite all appearances, with none of these instances were any differences in innate endowment involved, and that there are entirely satisfactory alternative explanations of the observed behaviours, the case for arguing that differences between individuals in their skills and abilities – even ones that are very substantial and apparent early in a child's life – form proof of the existence of innate gifts and talents would be seriously undermined.

The suggestion that inborn factors are the cause of the observed differences between certain European and African babies was addressed in a programme of research carried out in Kenya by Charles Super (1976). He studied the development of infants in a farming community of the Kipsigi tribe. Super's findings confirmed that Kipsigi infants do indeed gain motor skills such as walking, standing, and sitting without support about one month earlier than babies in other continents.

However, Super also observed that certain other skills, such as lifting the head, and crawling, are acquired later rather than earlier by Kipsigi babies, compared with other infants. These additional findings suggest that the forwardness of the African infants is specific to certain particular abilities. And most importantly, Super also showed that those skills that Kipsigi infants gain earlier than others are ones that are deliberately taught to them by Kipsigi mothers. In fact, their language contains specialized words that are called upon for the purpose of giving instruction in sitting and walking. When Super compared patterns of early crawling in different African tribes, he found that there was a substantial correlation (.77) between the proportion of the mothers who said they taught crawling to their babies and the average age at which crawling actually began. There was an even higher correlation (.90) between the availability of instruction and the age at which a baby began to crawl.

In the light of the evidence gathered by Super, it is almost certain that the reasons for the accelerated motor development observed in Kipsigi infants lie in cultural and environmental factors, and not inborn mechanisms. However, it is just conceivable that the explanation is that Kipsigi mothers happen to notice that their infants are 'naturally' good at certain skills and subsequently decide to encourage further progress in those particular areas of achievement. Fortunately, Super had data at hand for checking on this possibility. He was able to examine infants in families that shared the same genetic background as the babies with precocious motor skills, but had a different way of life, one that involved child-rearing practices that were more similar to European ones. He found that these infants, who did not receive the special training in motor skills received by infants living in the traditional villages, did not display any precocity at all at the skills at which the traditionally raised infants excelled. This further evidence confirms that the African infants' superior early progress at sitting, standing, and walking is caused by training and experience, not by inborn qualities.

In the case of the second example, the individual who could recall enormous lists of digits, he happened to be a male student who participated in an experiment in which he was paid to practise recalling digit lists for an hour every day over a two-year period (Chase and Ericsson, 1981). When the experiment commenced, his performance was no better than average. The fact that he eventually became quite exceptional was the consequence not of an innate talent but of his having received exceptional opportunities to practise the skill, over the two-year duration of the study.

The third example of a person with a remarkable skill, the man who was so exceptionally good at identifying briefly presented visual arrays, was someone who happened to be employed as a technician on a project using visual stimuli to investigate people's cognitive skills (Ceci *et al.*, 1987). It was his job to prepare the visual arrays that were used in the study. In the course of having to produce the materials needed for an experiment, he gained, informally, the equivalent of literally thousands of practice trials at the skill that was to be tested.

As for the five-year-old child who was so remarkably competent at swimming and controlling a canoe, the child happened to be a member of the Manu tribe in New Guinea (Mead, 1975). These people live in houses that are set on stilts above tidal lagoons. All the young children spend much of their time in or near the water, where they are encouraged to play, and they have countless opportunities to watch older children practise their skills. As a result of the children's particular early experiences, by the time they are about three years old virtually all have gained the skills that strike uninformed observers from land-based societies as being so remarkable – so much so that an observer who was unfamiliar with the special features of that culture would assume that special inborn gifts must have been involved.

The repeated demonstrations that children and adults can differ enormously in the capabilities they acquire for reasons that have nothing to do with innate talents do not conclusively prove that such talents are fictions, of course. However, they do make it clear that the existence of innate talents cannot be taken for granted. And in view of the practical dangers of unfair discrimination that arise from reaching the conclusion that talents exert a key influence upon high abilities in the lack of firm evidence that they actually do, it is probably wise to take the view that they are *not* an essential cause of high abilities, at least until the relevant research findings on both sides of this issue can be more carefully examined.

Some tentative conclusions

This opening chapter has briefly examined three states of affairs that are often associated with the presence of high abilities.

First, training and hard work were considered. These receive closer attention in the chapters that follow, but it is already clear that they are extremely important. High achievements always depend upon diligent efforts, with expertise in many areas of accomplishment demanding an investment of thousands of hours commited to training and practice.

Second, making a good start by gaining basic skills earlier than usual can increase a person's chances of achieving high levels of success. And efforts to accelerate early learning can be highly successful, a point to which we shall return, especially in Chapter 3.

Third, the role of another frequently mentioned influence upon high abilities, innate gifts and talents, has not received the endorsement given to the importance of training and an early start. Although it is widely believed that innate talents are crucial ingredients of abilities at the highest levels, I have challenged that viewpoint, demonstrating that certain manifestations of exceptional skills that appear to be inexplicable unless the roles of gifts and talents are acknowledged, can actually be explained quite differently. Like the other issues raised in the present chapter, gifts and talents will be re-examined later, in Chapter 7.

The book's contents

In the chapters that follow, various aspects of high abilities are investigated. *Chapter 2* examines the influences of a young person's family and home background. Some of the influential factors introduced in the present chapter are more closely examined, and various other family-related issues are discussed.

Chapter 3 concentrates on the findings of a number of studies designed to explore the possibility of accelerating young children's progress in various areas of ability.

Chapter 4 is about child prodigies. That chapter investigates the possible implications and consequences for a child of having been a prodigy, examining the connections between early progress and mature achievements.

Chapter 5 concerns geniuses, the highest achievers of all.

In *Chapter 6* I enquire into the possible relationships between impressive capabilities and measured intelligence.

In *Chapter 7*, the underlying causes of high abilities and expertise are examined. As well as considering the possible involvement of innate influences in the particular forms of gifts and talents, the chapter examines alternative ways in which genetic sources of individual variability may contribute to the fact that people vary as much as they do in their capabilities and their accomplishments.

Finally, *Chapter 8* raises a number of questions concerning the roles of parents in helping young people to learn.

Chapter 2

Family backgrounds

Home and family backgrounds affect young people in numerous ways. Families differ greatly in the extent to which they
value and encourage intellectual activities, and in the degree to
which pursuits that have a broadly educational function are
given priority. Families also vary in the kinds of role models
they provide. Also, they differ in the degree to which they give
a child opportunities to identify with successful individuals.

Of course, some children thrive despite being brought up in
apparently unfavourable home circumstances, and others fail
to achieve in spite of the fact that their families seem to have
provided highly stimulating early environments. But by and
large, young people do strongly benefit from the kinds of
encouragement and stimulation that conscientious parents can
provide (Wachs and Gruen, 1982). This chapter starts with
some research findings that demonstrate just how influential a
child's home and family background can be.

The influence of the family

Many studies have confirmed that language development in
children is related to their parents' social class (Hart and Risley,
1995). Researchers Betty Hart and Todd Risley conducted a
study designed to help explain why that is. These investigators
wanted to unravel the reasons for youngsters from professional families making faster progress at gaining language
skills than children whose parents are not so well educated.
Hart and Risley decided to simply count the sheer number of
words that were directed towards children in different home

backgrounds. They only counted those words that were specifically targeted towards a child. So, for example, the words in a conversation between adults in the child's home were not included, and nor were the ones a child might have heard on a television programme.

Hart and Risley had expected that they would find some differences between different social classes in the number of words directed towards children. However, they were staggered to discover how large the differences actually were. In just one week the number of words three-year-old children from varying social classes experienced differed, on average, by as much as 15 000. And by that age the children's total experiences of language directed towards them had already varied enormously. By this time a child from one of the professional families participating in the study would have experienced, on average, as many as 30 million words. Children from working-class families had heard around 20 million words. But children who came from families on welfare had only experienced about 10 million words directed towards them.

In other words, underlying the observed differences between children from varying social classes in their *progress* at language were huge differences in their home *experiences* of language. Of course, other influences, such as genetic differences between the children, may also have contributed to their varying competence, but the enormous variations in their actual experiences were almost certainly a major factor.

Studies of Nobel prizewinners have provided additional evidence of the importance of family backgrounds. Nobel prizes acknowledge excellence of various kinds, and only the most outstanding contributions are honoured in this manner. So it would clearly be useful to know about the family backgrounds of prizewinners. Information concerning this has been collected in studies by Harriet Zuckerman (1977) and by Colin Berry (1981; 1990). These researchers examined the cultural origins of around 400 prizewinning scientists.

Berry found that the impacts of family backgrounds were not at all hard to detect. The families of Nobel scientists have been much more frequently Protestant than Catholic, and individuals from Jewish home backgrounds have been Nobel prizewinners far more often than either Protestants or

Catholics. National differences as such have been relatively unimportant compared with differences in religious and cultural traditions. But irrespective of their country of origin, the vast majority of Nobel scientists have come from professional and business families. Also, within the professions certain occupational groups have contributed out of all proportion to their numbers. For example, the fathers of about 40 per cent of science prizewinners from professional backgrounds have either held university posts or have been medical doctors.

There are some interesting differences in the home backgrounds of science and non-science prizewinners. For example, over 30 per cent of winners of a Nobel Literature Prize experienced loss of a parent in childhood or adolescence, or family bankruptcy or impoverishment, but family tragedies in the early lives of prizewinning scientists have been less common, with the homes of Nobel scientists tending to be considerably more stable. Contrasting with the popular image of the 'great scientist' as a person who has triumphed in spite of having little schooling (like Michael Faraday) or an interrupted education (like Albert Einstein), the childhoods and early careers of the majority of eminent scientists were not affected by serious disruptions.

Of course, intriguing as these findings are, they are inevitably inconclusive concerning the actual causes of prizewinners' excellence: they raise more questions than they answer. They do not tell us to what extent the relationships between achievement and home background reflect genetic rather than cultural influences. There are other questions, too. Is a family's sheer wealth a crucial factor? Do certain 'elite' schools in large cities have a special importance? A cultured home background may provide successful role models, access to books, encouragement, good schooling, and high expectations, but are all of these equally advantageous?

Broadly speaking, each of the various ways in which families can stimulate children to excel at the capabilities that high achievements build upon falls into one of two broad categories. First, families help children to gain essential knowledge, skills, and mental strategies. Unsurprisingly, the ways in which children develop in their early years are affected by the degree to which the parents assume the role of a teacher or guide. For instance, a mother who encourages her daughter to read at an early age may be contributing to an explosive growth in the child's capabilities, because becoming literate can open up numerous new opportunities for a young person.

Second, family members transmit to a child their own values and their attitudes towards those kinds of achievements that depend upon learning and practice. The experiences of a young person who is exposed to lifestyles in which scholarly activities are enjoyed and respected, and who is given chances to witness the successful outcomes of sustained efforts to learn new skills, will bring advantages that are denied to many children.

How families influence children

Providing stimulation

How is the development of young people's abilities affected by family background? As was evident in the studies of Nobel prizewinners mentioned earlier, the effects of the home background have been seen especially clearly in the achievements of children from Jewish families, who have made contributions out of all proportion to their numbers. Before the Second World War, at least 20 per cent of Germany's scientists and mathematicians were Jewish, as were as many as half the mathematicians in Italy, although Jews made up less than 2 per cent of those countries' populations. In Britain and the Soviet Union, Jews have been similarly over-represented in science and the professions. Jewish scholars, artists, and professional people are equally prominent in the United States.

There are a number of contributing factors. One is a respect for scholarly activities, coupled with a keen awareness of the importance of education. Laszlo Polgar, the father of three chess-playing daughters who all achieved the quite remarkable feat of gaining Grandmaster status at chess in their teens, has noted that the Jewish religion prescribes for parents to teach their children from an early age, with the Talmud specifying that the parents should be the child's first teachers (Lennon, 1989). There is nothing new about Jewish appreciation of scholarship: in a list of important European scholars that was compiled before the year 1400, the proportion of Jews was three times their numerical frequency. Religious Jews have always held Talmudic scholars in high regard. Even on the Sabbath, when many activities are prohibited or restricted, study has not been discouraged. Another factor is the traditional importance attached to children in the family. Compared with families from other cultural origins, Jewish families have tended to be small and stable, with relatively few divorces. Consequently most Jewish children have benefited from the presence of having two parents at home. Many Jewish families in North America have lived in relatively affluent urban or suburban environments, where schools provide good cultural opportunities and have high expectations. Jewish children have been strongly encouraged to direct their energies towards the kinds of activities that lead to success at school.

Many other cultural traditions contain features that encourage early learning. In the Orient, for instance, children are taught to be unquestioningly obedient to their parents and to be attentive to teachers and other adults. As a result, the children of cultured parents often make fast early progress. The effects of combining a cultural tradition of submission to parental demands with expert teaching by an enthusiastic parent can be seen in the achievements of Yo-Yo Ma, a young Chinese cellist of exceptional ability who was also a remarkable prodigy in early childhood. At that time,

> Hiao-Tsiun [the father] tutored his children in French history, Chinese history, mythology, and calligraphy... and Yo-Yo took up the piano and the cello... No more than a short assignment was given daily, but this was to be thoroughly assimilated. He proceeded systematically and patiently. Each day, Yo-Yo was expected to memorize two measures of Bach; the following day, two more measures... By the time he was five, he had learned three Bach suites. (Blum, 1989, p. 48)

The combined effects of high parental expectations and a plentiful supply of encouragement to learn, as well the presence of scholarly role models and parents' eagerness to ensure that a child not only has opportunities to gain abilities but also devotes considerable amounts of time to study, can create an emotional and intellectual atmosphere in which it may appear difficult *not* to succeed. In certain instances one gains the impression that parents have convinced themselves even before their son (but rarely their daughter) is born, that the child will become a genius. Leo Wiener, the father of the great mathematician Norbert Wiener, seems to have had this expectation, which was certainly fulfilled (Wiener, 1953). So too did the parents of Yehudi Menuhin, whose father gave up his post as a teacher in order to concentrate on helping his children's careers. Both Menuhin parents firmly believed that every so often a brilliant child would be born into their family, and they seem never to have doubted that their son was destined for greatness (Rolfe, 1978). Similarly, John Maynard Keynes, who does not seem to have been outstandingly able as a young child, despite the fact that his mother worried about him working his brain too hard even before he reached the age of two, is described by his biographer as having been surrounded by 'the conviction that he was bound to be clever' (Skidelsky, 1983, p. 67) on the part of parents and other relatives. They would have been surprised and disappointed had he not turned out to be unusually capable.

Prophecies of this kind tend to be self-fulfilling. Parents sometimes convince themselves that a child is inherently talented after observing the child respond in a manner which is actually quite normal but which the parents believe to be indicative of extraordinary early development. And once the parents have got it into their heads that the child is specially gifted they start to act differently themselves. A probable consequence of that is to ensure that the child is exposed to those kinds of experiences and opportunities that do accelerate his or her abilities. The fact that the same 'special' treatment would have accelerated the development of many children who were never deemed to be specially talented is not always appreciated.

The early anticipations of a child's future achievements that can act as self-fulfilling prophesies are certainly not confined to Jewish families. Mozart's father had very definite ideas about his son's future career well before the child was weaned. The parents of the great nineteenth-century art critic and thinker

John Ruskin appear to have decided for themselves very early in his life that their child was going to be a quite exceptional person (Burd, 1973). The mother of the architect Frank Lloyd Wright decided in advance of his birth that her son was going to be a great architect, and she arranged for her infant to be surrounded by architectural images and pictures. John Stuart Mill has been said to have had genius drummed into his head by the relentless efforts of his father. In each of these cases the parents' expectations were largely fulfilled, and their efforts were amply rewarded. But in a number of instances the child had to pay a big cost. The inevitable pressure to succeed, and the emotional intensity of life in the kind of family that has such expectations, can have psychologically crippling effects.

Of course, not all cultural experiences and opportunities are mediated through the home and the family. Historical events may disrupt or outweigh the influence of family traditions. One series of investigations charted the progress of men who were born at the beginning of the present century, and whose lives were adversely affected at the start of their careers by the Great Depression, and again in mid career by the Second World War. The achievements of these people were found to be impaired in a number of ways compared with those of other men whose date of birth precluded historical events having such a negative influence (Elder, 1988; Elder *et al.*, 1989).

Giving structure and support

Stimulation and encouragement are clearly important for a growing child, but are they enough? Some recent investigations have shown that, at least for older children, additional elements of effective home backgrounds are equally crucial.

By early adolescence young people's continuing progress depends upon their having gained good working and studying habits. Among a group of young adolescents who are equally intelligent and promising, some are much more successful than others at forging ahead. A major reason is simply that some of these young people spend much more time than others at their studies. They engage in training and rehearsing activities more frequently, and they are more successful at concentrating on the learning activities that lead to competence. In other words, some adolescents are simply better than others at getting on with the job of learning. Their effectiveness at doing that makes an important contribution to their being unusually successful.

But why is that while some young people are capable of the studying and learning activities that lead to expertise and impressive abilities, other intelligent youngsters appear unable to do whatever it takes in order to extend their abilities? To answer that question, researcher Mihaly Csikszentmihalyi conducted a two-part study (Csikzentmihalyi and Csikszent-mihalyi, 1993).

Csikszentmihalyi and his colleagues had noticed that the majority of adolescents do not much enjoy the practising and studying activities that are necessary for getting ahead. Study-ing tends to be solitary and requires concentrated effort, and adolescents do not particularly like doing effortful things on their own. That is especially true of activities that require persistence at concentrated solitary work. Adolescents prefer to spend their time in other ways. They like to hang around with their friends, for example, or watch television, and engage in the activities that adolescents do enjoy. Studying is close to being their least favoured activity.

But as we have seen, studying is the key to success. You have to do it in order to make good progress. So it would be extremely helpful to know how and why those adolescents who do not greatly dislike studying differ from those who do. What is special about those young people who *can* study effectively?

In order to investigate this, Csikszentmihalyi needed to devise a way to assess how young people actually experience what they are doing at a particular time. He developed a technique that involved individuals carrying around with them a small bleeper. This bleeper would sound, on ten occasions every day, at randomly timed intervals. The instructions to the participants were to make entries into a little booklet they had been supplied with, whenever that happened. In the booklet there were a number of short questions to be answered each time the bleeper sounded. They asked about a youngster's activity at the time. One question queried what the young person was doing, and others asked where he or she was at the time, whether they were on their own or in company, and so on. Most importantly, one of the questions that had to be answered whenever a young person's bleeper sounded inquired into whether the participant was *enjoying* whatever he or she was engaged in. Another asked about the participants level of *alertness*.

Csikzentmihalyi discovered that if the bleeper happened to buzz at a time when an adolescent was studying, ratings on these latter two items tended to be very low. That is, the participants reported that they were *not* enjoying studying, and they were *not* feeling alert or attentive. But there were some adolescents whose responses at times when they were bleeped while studying were more positive. How did these individuals differ from the others?

It was possible to answer that question because the adolescents had been divided into four groups on the basis of information the researchers had obtained about their home and family backgrounds. The participants' backgrounds were rated on two dimensions. First, the home backgrounds were assessed in terms of the extent to which they were mentally *stimulating*. This dimension referred to the extent to which parents provided opportunities to learn and held high educational expectancies for their child. As we have already seen, it is extremely helpful for a young person to have a stimulating home background.

However, although being stimulating is a necessary attribute of a home background, it may not be a sufficient one. In the study the family backgrounds were also rated on another dimension that the researchers judged to be important. This second dimension referred to the extent to which families were rated as being *supportive*. With this measure, the participants were rated on the extent to which their family backgrounds provided them with help and structure. A family in which there were clear rules and clearly allotted tasks, and in which the children could depend upon one another, was rated as being a supportive one. In such families, young people knew what they had to do and usually got on with it. In contrast, a family in which structured support was unavailable or unreliable tended to be one in which young people spent a lot of their energy complaining or arguing. In such families, children tended to waste time and say things like 'its not fair', 'it's not my turn' rather then directing their attention to actual tasks and getting things done.

On the basis of the information available, each adolescent's family background was placed in one of four categories: neither stimulating nor supportive, supportive but not stimulating, stimulating but not supportive, or both supportive and stimulating. It was now possible to discover whether their category membership had an influence on how the adolescents responded to these questions about how they were experiencing studying.

So far as *non*-study activities were concerned (such as talking to friends or watching television), Csikzentmihalyi and his co-researchers found that the adolescents' responses to questions about their enjoyment of the activities and their attentiveness to them were not much affected by family background. In other words, there were no major differences between young people allotted to the four family background categories. But when the participants were asked to report how they were experiencing the activity of studying, there was considerable variation. In three of the four groups, their responses were, as I have already implied, very negative. These young people definitely did not enjoy studying, and their level of alertness when engaged in study activities was very low.

But one group was very different. They reported more favourable feelings about studying, and they also said they were more alert than the other participants when they were buzzed at a time when they were engaged in study activities. That group of participants consisted of the young people who belonged to the category in which family backgrounds were both supportive *and* stimulating. Adolescents from these family backgrounds, but not the others, were relatively positive about studying. They enjoyed it more, and when they were studying alone they reported being much more alert than the other young people.

So this research has identified two vital ingredients of family backgrounds. Being stimulating is one of them, but stimulation alone is insufficient. Being structured and supportive is also necessary, but that too is not enough on its own. It is the combination of these two attributes that is crucial. The young people whose home backgrounds were both stimulating and supportive had a big advantage over the others, making them more likely to succeed. These individuals had been helped to learn to get on with the job of studying, and that was yielding them real benefits. Of course, the advantages may have been temporary, rather than permanent. It is entirely possible that those young people who were not so fortunate in their backgrounds would have caught up later, but for the time being they were definitely at a disadvantage.

Mechanisms of family influence: the Chicago studies

The value of experiencing the combination of both stimulation to learn on the one hand and family support and structure on the other is evident from other research examining the backgrounds of young people who have made themselves unusually capable at a valued skill. Some useful insights into the particular ways in which families can help a young person to gain exceptional abilities have been provided by a series of large-scale investigations examining the early lives of children who, by the time they had become young adults, had already become remarkably accomplished in various areas of expertise. The investigations were undertaken by a group of researchers at the University of Chicago, headed by Benjamin Bloom (1985). In these studies information about family life and early childhood experiences was obtained from interviewing the exceptional young people themselves and also talking to their parents and the teachers who were involved in their early upbringing. The Chicago-based investigations included several separate but related studies. One looked into the early family lives of distinguished young mathematicians. Other studies investigated the backgrounds of young concert pianists, tennis champions and Olympic swimmers, sculptors, and neurologists.

What were the characteristics of these individuals' early home lives? Broadly speaking, the family backgrounds contained the very combination of considerable stimulation to learn and a high degree of support and structure that was highlighted in Csikzentmihalyi's investigations. The findings showed that in most cases the family was intact throughout the young person's childhood, and that the parents were willing to go to enormous lengths to help the individual to do well. The parents often supervised homework, and sometimes checked or inspected it. In most cases, especially when the child was young, a parent would happily attend any special lessons outside school and also be present at practice sessions.

As a rule, these parents placed considerable value on success. Most of them were themselves hard working and energetic people who favoured active over passive pursuits and considered it very important to achieve the very best that one could do. Passive interests such as watching television were not much encouraged by these parents. Family life tended to be firmly structured, with the children required to accept responsibilities and share household chores. The children were expected to learn to use their time efficiently enough to fit in a variety of daily activities: in these families, time was definitely not to be wasted. The parents were always willing to devote their own time and energy to their children – playing games, reading to them, or teaching or guiding them in one way or another.

The families interviewed in the Chicago studies differed from each other in many ways, but virtually all placed a high value on achieving. They made their children aware of the importance the parents attached to doing one's best. For most of the young people, it was the parents who first introduced them to the talent area in which they eventually excelled. Often, although not always, this coincided with a special interest of at least one of the parents. In consequence, the children almost always began developing special skills in the context of home activities. Typically, the parents provided appropriate teaching, usually of an informal kind, whenever a child showed particular interest. In this way, the child was progressively encouraged to participate in activities valued by the parents, and helped to acquire necessary knowledge and skills.

In short, whatever the particular area of expertise, the child's early interest in it came about as a fairly predictable consequence of living in the particular cultural milieu of that individual's everyday family life.

Even when learning resources outside the family were called upon, for teaching the piano or giving instruction in swimming or tennis, for example, the parents did not simply leave things to the teacher. Typically, they took upon themselves the responsibility to make sure that the child practised regularly (in most cases at least once per day), prepared carefully for lessons, and worked hard at learning new skills. These parents all seem to have realized that young children cannot be expected to practise alone at a repetitive activity. They were willing to spend time with their child, giving help and encouragement in one form or another, or making the practice session into a game. As one mother remarked, that was particularly helpful, because it is hard for a young child just to sit down and practise without someone to give encouragement (Sloane, 1985, p. 456). The Chicago studies report no evidence of any families of talented young people either having failed to provide a considerable amount of support or having lacked at least a modicum of interest in the talent area.

Recent investigations into the early background of competent young musicians in Britain have produced very similar findings (Sloboda and Howe, 1991). By no means all the parents in that series of studies had strong musical interests themselves, but they almost all were highly supportive and encouraging. Most of them helped their children to practise, and maintained contact with the teacher or even sat in on lessons. The teachers, too, were generally highly encouraging and good at getting on with their pupils. There was considerable emphasis on motivating the young people to do well.

In an area of expertise such as music it is easy to see why it is so beneficial for a child to have parents who provide help and encouragement with practising. Frequent and regular deliberate practice is absolutely essential if a child is going to make the early progress that is necessary in order for a child to achieve a high standard of performance by early adulthood. But for the majority of young children, practising is not an intrinsically attractive activity. In most cases the necessary practising simply won't get done unless there is a helpful adult to give the kind of support and assistance a parent can provide. Even among the highly successful young musicians interviewed by Sloboda and Howe (1991), most of them frankly admitted that had their parents not helped them in this way, they simply would not have done the practising that enabled them to have forged ahead. In other words, for these young people, the fact that the parents were so supportive was more than simply helpful; it was an essential ingredient of the children's success.

Distinguishing between environment and experience

Of course, although a child's home and family are important influences, these do not entirely determine how a young person develops, as is evident from the fact that two children brought up by the same parents often turn out very differently. Why is that?

There are a number of reasons. A particularly important consideration is the fact that what is most crucial about a child's surroundings is not the environment as such but the particular individual's actual *experiences* of that environment. That is an essential distinction that people often fail to make, neglecting to distinguish between differences in children's environments and differences in their experiences.

There is a tendency to assume that similar environments produce similar experiences, but that is only true to a limited extent. In reality, two children brought up in the identical family environment may have remarkably dissimilar experiences, as is evident from the findings of research into siblings that has been conducted by Judy Dunn and Robert Plomin (1990).

These investigators have demonstrated that two children who are reared in broadly the same environment may nevertheless have sharply contrasting early experiences. This happens even when the parents of two small children attempt to arrange things so that the children are treated as equitably as possible. Imagine a family in which the parents make big efforts to do that. Each child is given the same amount of attention, and the same amount of support, and the conscientious parents do their best to make sure that the children have opportunities to engage in the same activities.

Yet, despite these efforts on the part of the parents, the two children will almost certainly report experiencing their childhoods very differently. Why is that? One of the commonest reasons is that in a typical family, one child, who is in the position of being the older one, perceives herself as having been brought up far less indulgently than the younger sibling. The older child is likely to feel that more has been demanded of her. The other child, being younger, is equally likely to feel sharply aware of being deprived of what she sees as the older sibling's privileges. For instance, the young child notices that compared with her older sister she has had to go to bed earlier. Also, she may feel that she has been deprived of the opportunities given to her sibling to engage in exciting activities like eating with a knife and playing with scissors.

In short then, despite all the parents' efforts to provide an environment that is the same for each child, these attempts fail to ensure that the two children have equivalent experiences, because of the unavoidable fact that one child experiences life from the perspective of the older sibling and the other sees things from the viewpoint of the younger. Whatever the parents do by way of ensuring that their children are raised in similar environments, they simply cannot guarantee that two children will have identical experiences.

It is important to keep in mind this important distinction between experience and environment. It is relatively easy to produce measures of a child's environment, and such measures can certainly be useful. But we must remember that measures of environment are not measures of experience, and it is the latter, not the former, that is the really crucial influence upon a child's life.

Sex and gender differences

There are few areas of human achievement in which men have not predominated. In a man's world, men have usually held the power to decide which kinds of achievement are to be valued. Males have dominated politics and religion, finance and industry, as well as the arts and the sciences, and men have always taken most of the Nobel prizes. Writing of Einstein, one psychologist has remarked 'if little Albert had been a girl, I think we would never have heard of her' (Feldman, 1986, p. 172). All the same, however, some women have managed to succeed. Everyone has heard of Marie Curie and Charlotte Brontë.

For most children, even today, the family provides the setting in which boys and girls begin to be treated differently. From a very early age they are encouraged to have contrasting, sex-related, interests. Father Christmas does not hand out guns to little girls or dolls to small boys. Sex-related differences in the activities and behaviours that win parental approval can be seen even in the earliest years. And most girls are still encouraged to take an interest in the skills that make a woman into a good homemaker, whereas very few boys are expected to gain expertise at cleaning, cooking, sewing, knitting, and taking care of babies. In many families, a girl's experiences will lead her to see herself as a future wife and mother, who is expected to support her husband's efforts to succeed in his career, but whose own working activities outside the home are confined to jobs that are considered 'suitable' for women.

In a study of the early experiences of great mathematicians, William Fowler (1986) found that three of the six women in his sample had encountered severe opposition to their careers from their families. Even now it remains true that many jobs held by women are ones that are poorly paid, with limited opportunities for advancement. As Virginia Woolf observed, it is no accident that from well before Jane Austen's time until the present day, the writing of good novels, an enterprise that can, at a pinch, be squeezed in between clearing up after one meal and preparing the next one, has been one of the few areas of creative endeavour at which substantial numbers of women have been highly successful.

So the disadvantaged status of women is by no means a thing of the past. Nor is it confined to poorly educated groups. Even today, many women do not have enough control over their lives to be able to pursue their interests with the single-mindedness and dedication, or the firm sense of direction, that is encountered in men who win Nobel prizes or reach other pinnacles of acknowledged achievement outside the home. The following quotation from a young college woman polled in the 1970s is still not entirely untypical.

My father even has a little bell he rings and my mother comes running and brings him coffee and he will call her from another room to change the television station. And it has been so successful. He is so happy and she is happy doing it. Why not treat him like a king because the male ego is kind of a sensitive thing to go tampering with? My life is probably not going to make that much difference on society, but maybe what my husband and children do will. I don't feel that I am that important. (Hayes, 1981)

Even those women who, unlike the young lady just quoted, do have a serious desire to do well may find themselves stopped in their tracks by restrictive parental attitudes. David Feldman reported the bitter experience of a young woman who had been a talented young pianist but whose religious parents believed that

> it was a sin for a little girl to have such a passion for mastering the instrument. For several years this woman fought a titanic battle with her parents over her music. She was forbidden to practise and was kept inside to prevent her from finding a piano elsewhere... After several years of this, her endurance waned and she finally gave up... Now in her fifties, the pain and sadness of her story were still evident. (Feldman, 1986, p. 183)

The outcome of within-family differences in the extent to which boys and girls are encouraged to succeed at non-domestic accomplishments has been to deny certain opportunities to many women. The cultural and environmental factors that lead to between-family differences in the extent to which children are encouraged to succeed are in many respects similar to the within-family sex differences that exist in the way boys and girls are treated.

Patterns of interaction in the earliest years

A large body of research has examined the relationships between children's development and various aspects of the home background (Wachs and Gruen, 1982; Gottfried, 1984). Because infants are not identical, even at birth, it is impossible to prescribe in fine detail the kinds of maternal childraising practices that are most effective for getting a young child started on a path leading towards being highly competent. Much depends upon the needs and temperament of the particular child. Moreover, the parents' effectiveness at aiding a baby's progress depends only to a limited extent on the choice of 'good' child rearing practices. Sensitivity to the particular needs of the individual baby is more crucial. The sensitive mother is good at perceiving her baby's state at a given moment, and discerning the infant's current requirements.

Researchers have obtained a substantial body of evidence concerning the ways in which mothers act towards their infants. The sensitivity of the mother to her young infant's signals appears to be a crucial factor in determining the infant's progress towards becoming able to communicate effectively with other people. In one series of investigations, it was discovered that by the end of the first year those infants whose mothers were rated as being highly sensitive to their needs were found to have made more progress than the other babies at acquiring certain other abilities that are essential for intellectual and social development (Ainsworth *et al.*, 1974).

Findings such as the above ones indicate that differences in mothering undoubtedly do affect infants' progress, although it is not entirely clear to what extent patterns of early mother–infant interaction influence an individual's eventual competence, as an adult. It is reasonable to suppose that those young infants whose mothers are highly sensitive to their needs are more likely to become intellectually outstanding adults than infants whose mothers are less sensitive. But practical difficulties make it hard to either verify or disprove the assertion that there are inevitable long-term consequences. One problem is that those mothers who are highly sensitive to the needs of their one-year-olds tend also to continue to be aware of the needs of the same children when they are three years old, five years old, and so on. In principle, it would be possible to devise a suitable experimental procedure for measuring the effects of early mother–infant patterns of interaction as such, without the confounding effects of subsequent events. This could be achieved by assessing a large sample of individuals whose mothers were induced to act with varying (and carefully measured) sensitivity towards their children in different years. In practice, for obvious ethical reasons, it is not possible to do this.

Most of the findings emerging from investigations based on observations of interactions between a mother and her child take the form of correlations indicating the size of the relationships between the behaviours of mother and infant. The inevitable limitation of this kind of evidence is that one can rarely be certain that a cause and effect influence is involved. The findings suggest that differences in mothers' behaviours may affect their babies, although alternative explanations cannot be ruled out. Partly for this reason, and partly because of the uncertainty about the long-term effects of the qualities of childrearing that are found to affect children's progress in the short term, we would not be justified in making confident predictions about the contributions of someone's experiences in early infancy to that individual's chances of becoming an extraordinarily competent adult.

How crucial are the earliest years of life?

Questions about the long-term psychological effects (if there are any) of a child's upbringing during early infancy lead to queries about the possibility that there are certain 'critical periods' in early life. Underlying the concept of a critical period is the view that if an event does not occur at a particular time in the child's early life, the developmental progress that is normally caused by that event will either never take place at all or be permanently abnormal or incomplete.

From birth onwards, much of what a young child learns is acquired when the child is interacting with an adult. Inevitably, the child's main caretaker – who is usually but not always the biological mother – has a major influence on what a baby learns in the earliest years. But just how important are those early years for a child's future achievements? Are the first months and years absolutely critical, in which case a mother's failure to provide an ideal early learning environment will restrict the child's progress in later years, ruling out development beyond a certain level? Or do the mother's activities during her baby's earliest years have a less crucial influence on the child's eventual intellectual development? And, in order to become a person who achieves extraordinary accomplishments, is it essential to have grown up with a caregiver who provided a good environment in the first years of life? Or is it possible to compensate for slow progress in the earliest years?

We are in no position to give really firm answers to the two final questions. The evidence simply is not available. To provide the essential data we would need to have detailed records of the early lives of a substantial number of outstanding people. But since such individuals form a very small minority of the children who are born, in order to obtain records of the earliest years of even a few individuals who are sufficiently exceptional to, say, win a Nobel prize, it would be necessary to collect detailed data on literally thousands of people.

Yet it is possible to at least take a stab at answering some of the questions. It is known that exceptional individuals have grown up in many different and widely varying historical periods. Between these times the values, customs and conventions surrounding childraising have altered enormously. So we can be fairly sure that the early upbringings of exceptional people have not all been similar. And a substantial number of brilliant people have emerged from family backgrounds that have been unhappy, or poverty-stricken, or in other ways far from ideal. Charlie Chaplin had an appalling childhood. His father was a heavy drinker, his mother was mentally unstable, and at the age of five the child was sent to an orphanage, where he stayed for two years. George Bernard Shaw's home background was far from perfect, and he complained (not entirely fairly) that his mother disliked and rejected him. The author Jack London's home life was particularly grim: and much of his late childhood, in California, was spent in places that were even worse than the blacking factory where the young Charles Dickens was forced to work. Isaac Newton's mother abandoned him when he was a young child, leaving him with his grandmother. The family of the great railway engineer George Stephenson was so poor that he never went to school at all.

So the possibility that the presence of a very specific pattern of 'ideal' mothering behaviour is an absolutely essential feature of the early background of outstanding individuals is definitely ruled out. On the other hand, there are no records of children who have suffered really severe deprivation of caregiving in their earliest years becoming adult geniuses. That is not to deny that there have been outstanding people who were deprived of their biological mothers, of course, but it would appear that in every case the child has had the opportunity to form a secure attachment with one or more caretakers.

Another possibility is that normal development will fail to occur unless learning take place at particular, 'critical' periods during the child's earliest years. There is a substantial amount of empirical evidence on this matter, although as with many other psychological questions, the fact that some evidence exists does not necessarily make it easy to provide simple answers. (Quite often, increases in knowledge simply heighten our awareness of the multiplicity of influences affecting human development, so that the reply to an apparently straightforward query has to begin with the phrase 'It depends upon…'.)

One question to which a definite answer can be given is that of whether there exist critical periods during babies' first months, when certain things have to be learned if they are to be acquired at all. For example, is a one-year-old who has been visually deprived, or prevented from hearing language, permanently impaired thereby? Here the answer is a definite 'No'. There do not appear to be critical periods for early development of human abilities that are as sharply defined as that. Children have a noteworthy ability to recover from severe early deprivations. But that is not to rule out the possibility of there being permanent retardation if physiological damage occurs (as can happen with certain eye disorders), or if the period of deprivation is very lengthy.

In summary, researchers have acquired a substantial body of information concerning the short-term effects of some of the ways in which mothers behave towards their babies. In the short term, maternal behaviours undoubtedly do affect the development of infants and young children. There is much less evidence about the long-term consequences of differences in mothering practices. All the same, and despite the lack of detailed findings concerning the childrearing practices of the mothers of outstanding individuals, the fact that maternal behaviour is known to affect development in the short term provides a degree of support for the view that the children of mothers who interact sensitively with their babies will eventually be more likely to reach extraordinary levels of achievement than the children of mothers whose childrearing behaviours are less effective. But the effects of differing standards of mothering are not the all-or-none ones that would be expected if there were firmly defined critical periods for intellectual development. They are not quite so fixed, or irreversible.

Effective mothering in early childhood will usually give a child a good start in life. In most cases that will have beneficial long-term consequences, partly through a kind of snowballing effect. Other things being equal, a child who, as a result of the mother's effectiveness as a teacher, gains useful abilities that facilitate the acquisition of further useful skills, will thereby have a definite advantage over less-favoured children. For example, a child who learns to speak comparatively early will thereby gain communicative skills that open up numerous opportunities to the young learner. And language, once acquired, encourages thinking and planning, and makes remembering possible. As one father observed 150 years ago,

> It is clear that the correct acquisition of his mother tongue makes the child intelligent at an early time, for it puts his attention and his several mental powers continuously in action. He is obliged always to search, distinguish, compare, prefer, report, choose, in short he must work, that is, think. (Witte, 1975, p. 75)

If the favourable circumstances are maintained over a long period, the effects will be cumulative. But circumstances can change, and a mother who is unusually effective at providing an optimal environment for her baby's earliest years may be less successful at providing support and encouragement for learning in later childhood.

What is good mothering? For a very sound reason, it is simply not possible to specify the precise mothering activities that will maximize the intellectual development of a child, or any other aspect of early child development. Because young babies vary so much – in temperament, cuddliness, activity level, and perceptual sensitivity, for instance – the kind of mothering activities that are maximally effective differ from one infant to another. So a pattern of mothering behaviours that is ideal for one baby will be much less suitable for a different child. It is largely for this reason that effective mothering is characterized not by particular ways of acting towards babies, but by the capacity to respond with considerable sensitivity to the unique needs of an individual child. There are no grounds for asserting that, to be effective, the mother should always behave in such-and-such a way.

The years following infancy: Feuerstein's insights

With studies of the family environments of toddlers and older children we are on much firmer ground. It is clear that a child's progress is strongly influenced by the kinds of activities and interactions that take place within the family. Differences between families in the ways in which language is used are especially crucial. Biographical information about the early lives of outstanding people often points to the parents moving heaven and earth to provide a child with rich early learning experiences. For instance, early in the seventeenth century, at a time when the majority of parents would not have been aware of the potential importance of educational experiences in early childhood, the father of Pascal, the mathematician, went to great lengths to provide intellectual stimulation for his three children. Pascal's father not only spent a large proportion of his own time with his children, but hired a substantial number of tutors to provide advanced instruction in fields outside his competence.

Biographical information about early family backgrounds is often fragmentary, and where it does exist it often takes the form of anecdotes which may be unreliable (Howe, 1982; Wallace, 1986). But the evidence does point to the presence of a parent or other relative who is strongly committed to giving help and encouragement in the early lives of many, and possibly most, of those people who have come to be regarded as being outstanding for their intellectual accomplishments.

That 'cultured' homes tend to produce highly educated young people is commonplace knowledge. To be really useful either for practical purposes or for adding to our understanding of the causes of extraordinary achievements, information about the characteristics of effective home environments needs to be more detailed and more precise. For example, how do parents in varying family backgrounds differ in the ways they behave towards their children? How do different parents cope with the task of teaching their sons and daughters new skills? Exactly what do good parents do that less effective parents fail to do? And why is it that even at the time they begin school, some young children are much better equipped than others with mental and social skills that make success likely, and are better at communicating and maintaining concentration? One fruitful source of insights has been the work of a psychologist whose main aim has been to discover why certain schoolchildren have *failed* to make normal progress.

Reuven Feuerstein, a psychologist working in Israel, was confronted with the learning difficulties experienced by many of the children of recent immigrants to that country. Although these children were in many respects sharp, quick, 'streetwise', and bright, they experienced severe problems with learning at school. However hard they tried, they seemed unable to solve school learning tasks, especially ones in which it was necessary to reflect on a problem before responding, or to categorize items, or keep material in memory. Children like these suffer from what Feuerstein terms 'reduced modifiability'. By this he means a lack of adaptability to new situations, and diminished ability to learn from experience (Feuerstein *et al.*, 1985; Howe, 1987).

Feuerstein (1980) discovered that the root cause of many of the difficulties experienced by the young people who were referred to him lay in their family lives during early childhood. The parents are a child's first guides to an initially unfamiliar world. Most parents spend a great deal of time in various activities that have the effect of passing on to the child a knowledge of the culture into which he or she is born. The precise form of that knowledge, and the way it is communicated, will vary enormously from culture to culture, but in one way or another parents and others act in ways that serve to pass on to the child an awareness of important cultural elements. These include information and activities of various kinds, in the form of customs, conventions, religious beliefs, and ways of behaving in a variety of situations. They also include a number of practical skills.

Teaching and guiding seem to be universal parental activities. Observations of parents and children living together in different societies throughout the world show that the ways in which parents talk to their offspring and interact with them, even in cultures that are technologically very primitive, are often remarkably similar to the patterns of interaction seen in 'advanced' cultures such as ours. And even in the most primitive societies, it is often clear that the parent has a deliberate *intention* to teach. Feuerstein asserts that parental intentionality has important consequences for the child's learning.

For example, when a Bushman trains his child to make a spear or a bow and arrow the parent displays his intentions by requiring the child to follow his actions and by deliberately slowing down his own rhythm of work. Each of these deliberate parental teaching procedures has the effect of increasing the likelihood that the child will be able to perceive how the various activities involved in the construction of a weapon contribute towards the eventual product.

As a result of the guidance and instruction received at home, by the end of childhood each individual will have acquired what he or she is expected to know in order to be a fully competent member of the cultural group. Instruction may be formal or informal, and the contexts in which knowledge is transmitted may include any combination of a variety of alternative activities, including story-telling, song, dance, many forms of play and games, other opportunities for imitation, festivities, ceremonies, rituals, and trials of strength. Diverse as human cultures are, they all have mechanisms which ensure that the growing child will interact with other people in ways that result in the child 'learning the culture' in which he or she grows up, and thereby becoming a competent member of the society.

When Feuerstein looked into the backgrounds of the children who were experiencing especially severe difficulties with school learning, he discovered that almost all of them came from families that had failed to provide the cultural learning experiences which form a normal part of the process of growing up. Typically, the parents were recent immigrants to Israel, from very different and technologically unsophisticated societies in the Near East and northern Africa. In Israel, they found it difficult to adjust to an unfamiliar and essentially westernized way of life, one which contrasted with the traditional cultures in which they had been raised. As confused newcomers to a strange new society which these parents were trying – with difficulty, and no great success – to understand, they thought that what they had learned in their own childhoods was of no value for life in modern Israel. Most importantly, so far as their children were concerned, the parents felt that they had little that was useful to pass on to the new generation, who would have to make their lives in a westernized modern state. Consequently, believing that what they had learned from their own parents would be useless for their children, these people failed to spend much time with their children or engage with them in the various activities through which, in other circumstances, the children would have learned about the traditional culture. These parents were not providing the guiding activities that their children needed. The children were therefore deprived of their parents' essential teaching and guidance.

A consequence of not having opportunities to interact with their parents in the many learning situations that occur naturally in a society where it is deemed necessary to pass on knowledge to the young, is that children also fail to acquire a number of basic learning and thinking skills, ones that pupils must have if they are to be at all successful at the kinds of learning tasks that are important at school. A child who never acquires these skills, which Feuerstein insists are essential prerequisites for school learning, is very seriously deprived, and can never catch up with others. Feuerstein believes that such a child is 'unmodifiable'. By this he means that the child is closed to the possibility of being altered by new experiences.

The fact that the significant deprivation in these children's lives is not in their lack of culture in its static aspects – knowledge, customs, and so on – but in their failure to experience the cultural processes by which knowledge, values, and beliefs are transmitted from one generation to the next, is illustrated by some apparently paradoxical contrasts in the differing capacities of various cultural groups to adapt to an unfamiliar way of life. Feuerstein compared the experiences of immigrants who came to Israel from the Yemen with those of immigrants from certain regions of northern Africa. Of the two groups, the Yemenites' traditional lives are much more remote from and different to the dominant western culture of modern Israel than are the lifestyles of the North Africans. Yet despite the greater difference between their traditional culture and Israeli culture, the Yemenite immigrants adapted to life in the unfamiliar modern society more rapidly and more effectively.

Feuerstein's explanation stems from his view that what is most vital, so far as successfully adapting is concerned, is not the degree of similarity between old and new environments but the degree to which the individuals are modifiable. This latter quality depends, as we have seen, upon the extent to which, through the family activities that lead to knowledge of a culture being gained, individuals have acquired the intellectual tools that underlie the capacity of a person to change, to adapt, and also to learn at school. As a consequence of possessing appropriate learning abilities and habits, people who, like the Yemenites, but unlike some of the other immigrants from northern Africa, have been brought up in highly developed societies – however remote or 'traditional' they may be – are generally able to adapt to the ways of an entirely new way of life.

If Feuerstein is right, an important lesson to be learned is that parents have an essential role as guides and interpreters for their children. They direct children's attention to those aspects of the everyday world that are especially significant. They encourage children to undertake the kinds of mental activities and strategies that will result in skills and knowledge being learned. In the absence of this guidance some forms of learning may be unimpeded, but other kinds of learning, especially those that require the sustained attention and reflective thinking that is often necessary in school learning tasks, will fail to occur.

Feuerstein asserts that children's need for such guidance is often underestimated. Many parents have been encouraged to believe that their children's intellects will develop satisfactorily so long as the environment is sufficiently rich, in the sense of being varied and stimulating. According to this view, all that is necessary is to ensure that there are plenty of interesting events for the child to perceive – for instance, sights and sounds that carry information from which the child can learn. Parents of young babies have been advised to hang mobiles above their infants' cots, and introduce stimuli that provide shapes, colours, and movement. The more lively, varied, and event-filled the child's environment, the more 'enriched' it is thought to be.

Unfortunately, however, that view is quite wrong. A stimulating physical environment may well be necessary, but this kind of stimulation on its own is very far from being sufficient to ensure that a child gains either knowledge or intellectual skills. As we have seen, it is also essential that the intellectual nourishment which the child's environment provides is channelled and interpreted to the child, or, to use Feuerstein's preferred term, *mediated*, by someone who can explain things, direct attention to what is important, and provide needed feedback for the child's own efforts to cope with various tasks.

One of Feuerstein's own examples provides a neat illustration of the way in which adults can help the child by mediating between him and the physical environment in a way that increases the child's understanding. He asks his readers to consider the difference between the two following instructions, each of which might be given by a parent to a young child,

1. Please buy three bottles of milk.
2. Please buy three bottles of milk so that we will have enough left over for tomorrow when the shops are closed.

Feuerstein points out that in the second instance, as distinct from the first, the child who complies with the instruction is not just carrying out a command. That child will also become involved in the reasoning that lies behind the request. As a result, the kind of understanding that is likely to accompany the action will include anticipating a set of conditions that may occur in the future, and a plan of activities that are designed to lead to the goal that guides the child's behaviour. And consequently, Feuerstein claims, 'the effects of such instructions are not limited to their specific contents but rather produce an orientation that may not be conceivable without exposure to mediation of this nature' (Feuerstein, 1980, p. 21).

With carefully mediated early stimulation, children can often acquire difficult skills several years before the age at which they are normally learned. But in the absence of the kinds of guidance and support that a caring parent can provide, the likelihood of a young child gaining certain key skills is minimal. However rich is a young child's environment in interest and variety, stimulation alone is never enough.

Problems of family life

Children can suffer as well as benefit from being brought up in a family environment where there is intense pressure to do well, or where the emphasis on the training of particular abilities leads to a child being deprived of important childhood experiences. It is not difficult to find signs of emotional stress that appears to have originated in the intense family atmospheres that parents who place great store on their children's success are prone to create. Norbert Wiener, the mathematician, found himself over-dependent on his parents and oppressed by the demands of a father who expected too much of his son. The great nineteenth-century critic John Ruskin's home atmosphere appears to have been equally intense, even claustrophobic. The fact that he was unable to detach himself from his over-controlling mother almost certainly contributed to the mental breakdowns that punctuated his life, and to his appalling behaviour towards his wife, Effie, who finally escaped from their six-year unconsummated marriage by running away with the painter John Everett Millais. And it is more than likely that had James Mill been less harsh and joyless, or a less grimly demanding father, his brilliant son John Stuart Mill would have been a warmer and perhaps happier adult. He might not have experienced the deep depression that almost drove him to suicide at the age of 20. In a number of talented families one gains the firm impression that parents and child have each become too dependent on the other, and at the same time resentful of this situation.

Even so, there are no firm grounds for believing that most parents who give their children unusually rich early learning experiences are either better or worse than other parents at helping their children to become happy and emotionally mature adults. The talented young people interviewed in the Chicago project gave every indication that their childhoods had been at least averagely happy. There is nothing in the interview responses to suggest that, as adults, they are noticeably neurotic or dissatisfied with their adult lives. Certainly, these people do seem to have experienced child-hoods that were in some respects unusually intense and demanding, and with a large competitive element. On the other hand, their family backgrounds seem mostly to have been warm and supportive, and parent–child relationships generally appear to have been close and mutually rewarding. Of course, it could be objected that the University of Chicago studies of talented young people examined only a particu-larly successful sample of those children whose parents have made special efforts to provide an enriched early environ-ment. Conceivably, there are other young people who have been stunted or damaged by constant exposure to all the pressures of life in an intense and over-demanding 'hot house' family atmosphere.

A central question is whether or not the numbers of talented and able people can be greatly enlarged. The answer is a clearly positive one: providing better early opportunities for early learning, particularly within the home context, can lead to large and permanent increases in achievements of many kinds. But raising the possibility that early family circum-stances might also have certain undesirable effects, in addition to the positive outcomes they are intended to achieve, reminds us that at the same time as we are considering evidence concerning the effectiveness of parental efforts to help their children progress, we must also keep in mind another ques-tion. That question asks whether or not adults *should* take various steps that are designed to increase their children's skills and achievements. It reflects a concern with the matter of whether it is proper for a parent to act in various ways, ones that may not simply affect the child's abilities, but may have other strong influences on the kind of person he or she will turn out to be.

Questions about the desirability of parents acting towards their children in ways that are special or unusual are often difficult to answer, partly because of lack of firm evidence, and partly because the desirable states to which the questions implicitly refer are hard to quantify. Happiness is not so easily assessed as success at objectively measurable achievements. The issues involve personal values, concerning which there is often no universal agreement. (How, for example, can we resolve questions such as, 'Is it better for a person to be a happy "failure" or a neurotic high-achiever?', and 'Is it better to have interests of many kinds or to be master of one particular field of endeavour?') Even the best parents may be too closely involved with the lives of their families to be in a position to consider questions about their own children's future happiness in anything like an objective or detached manner.

But hard as it is to address questions like these, we cannot afford to ignore them. They are far too important. Once it becomes apparent that procedures which are intended to extend a child's progress may have additional, conceivably undesirable consequences for the individual, it becomes clear that those questions, which enquire not what parental intervention can achieve but what parents ought to do in connection with a child's early education, must receive serious consideration. There are always psychological costs to be paid for gaining an extraordinary capability. Unfortunately, some parents are unable or unwilling to recognize that, for some children, the value of a particular achievement may not justify the emotional expense.

The different influences of family and school

The family background is not the only source of the child's learning experiences, of course. Schools have an influence, as well. After all, we spend much of our childhood at school, and schools are designed to help children gain important knowledge and skills. Is not the school, as a supplier of educational experiences, more important than the home?

For most children who grow up to be unusually able people, it is probably not. That is not to deny that parents and their children depend on schools to contribute a substantial proportion of the instruction that is necessary in order for young people to become educated. On the whole, schools do an excellent job with the resources that are available to them. They succeed in ensuring that almost all children become reasonably literate and numerate, with all sorts of knowledge and skills at their disposal.

But schools labour under the enormous disadvantage of having a small number of teachers to instruct a large number of children. This does not prevent schools from succeeding at the task of educating vast quantities of children to a level that is usually deemed to be satisfactory, nor does it prevent them providing the most able children with valuable educational experiences that complement home-based learning. However, the fact that each teacher has to work with a large number of children does have the effect of making it impossible to give each young child that wealth and intensity of experiences appropriate to the particular individual that the most stimulating home backgrounds can provide. On its own, a school can rarely succeed in giving the intellectual nourishment that results in a child excelling at something, rather than being merely competent.

Schools are undoubtedly essential, and the quality of the schooling they provide is undoubtedly important: the best schools can do a far more effective job than poorer schools (Rutter, 1989). Moreover, many successful people have spoken with warmth about the enormous positive influence of certain outstanding teachers. All the same, when we look for the reasons leading to some children, but not others, becoming extraordinarily able, more of those reasons will be related to differences in home backgrounds than to differing experiences at school. Parents who seek to discover what can be done to maximize the likelihood of their child becoming especially able find that most of the best opportunities for taking practical steps towards achieving this aim lie within the home and the family, not the school. Parents get to know their own children really well, as individuals. For schoolteachers, in contrast, the practical demands of their job make it impossible to have a comparable knowledge of the individual characteristics of every child they teach. Parents can work and play with their children on a one-to-one basis, if necessary for hours at a time. For the classroom teacher this is simply not possible. And for most parents who would like to help their children to become unusually capable adults, the positive effects of sending a child to a good school are far exceeded by those that can be achieved by the parents themselves spending time with the children and encouraging them to learn, and providing an interesting, attentive, and supportive home life.

Chapter 3

Accelerating the acquisition of children's abilities

To what extent is it possible to accelerate the acquisition of basic skills and capabilities by young children? Is attempting to do that desirable? If such acceleration is possible, are there undesirable side effects? Is it possible for ordinary adults to gain exceptional skills? These important questions are addressed in this chapter and the one that follows it. In the present chapter the emphasis is upon what can be achieved. The following chapter examines the roles of parents and others in encouraging children to extend their capabilities, and also raises questions about the desirability of attempting to accelerate development.

Gesell's studies of accelerated learning

Successive generations of psychology students have been told about a series of infant training experiments that were undertaken early in the twentieth century. It was widely reported that the findings showed that any effects of giving infants special training were short-lived, with the advantages tending to disappear within a matter of weeks. For example, when Gesell and Thompson (1929) gave one member of a pair of identical girl twins six weeks' training in climbing stairs (starting at 46 weeks), they reported that although the specially trained child gained a temporary advantage over the other twin, the advantage was wiped out after the second child had received just two weeks' training, which in her case began seven weeks later.

The finding that a child could catch up fairly easily if training was delayed for a few weeks was seen as providing support for Arnold Gesell's view of human development as largely an 'unfolding' process. Gesell believed that a person's eventual capabilities are essentially determined before birth. As a child grows, the physical maturation that takes place enables various abilities to unfold. Gesell thought that there was little point in trying to bring forward the development of skills before the stage at which the unfolding process makes the child ready to acquire them. At that time, but not before, according to Gesell, they are gained easily and naturally.

Gesell believed that his findings were consistent with his view that attempts to accelerate early progress would have no beneficial long-term effects. But a close examination of his actual results does not support this conclusion. In fact, as William Fowler (1983) discovered when he re-examined Gesell's data, certain of the results provide firm evidence that the early training sessions did, after all, have substantial long-term effects. Although Gesell had reported these results, he paid little attention to them and failed to draw the obvious conclusions, which would have contradicted the nativist beliefs he held.

Fowler noted that Gesell was correct to observe that on tasks at which one twin but not the other received very early training, the initially untrained twin, if taught the skill several months later, did make faster progress than the other twin had done. However, Fowler also noted that certain advantages were maintained by the twin who was trained first. For instance, that child's mastery of a manipulation task involving delicate control over toy blocks was never quite matched by the twin who learned the task later. In a later study in which the same twins again participated as experimental subjects, the child who was trained first did better at the vast majority of the skills they were taught. Her advantages were maintained in follow-up tests administered four weeks and 12 weeks after the second twin had received training. Even when the twins were teenagers, the twin who received earlier training in climbing stairs was still superior at a number of motor skills, including running, walking, and tap-dancing. Also, even after the twins had entered adolescence, the first child maintained her advantage in important language skills such as pronunciation and sentence construction. She also had a larger vocabulary.

What is more, the twin taught earliest maintained her superiority despite the fact that the actual duration of the training was relatively short. Stair-climbing, for instance, was taught for only 20 minutes per day, over a six-week period. So it appears that what Gesell's findings actually confirm – despite his own very different interpretation of them – is that a relatively brief period of early training can be enough to induce a permanent improvement.

Another sign of Gesell's apparent blindness to the influences of early experience was his failure to notice that the progress of *both* twins on the skills at which they had received training was well ahead of developmental norms. Fowler pointed out that the average American child, according to data collected by Gesell himself, cannot walk up stairs with assistance until around 18 months, and only walks unaided at two years. Yet in the twin study, even the child who was given less training, totalling fewer than five hours over a two-week period, could climb five stairs alone in about ten seconds at the age of one year. In view of the fact that the training given to the twins was always short in duration and never involved more than a small fraction of the day, the finding that early training did have long-lasting effects provides rather strong evidence of the importance of early experience. The fact that, even so, there were clear differences between the twins, despite both of them having been given special training, makes it fair to suggest that had the studies compared the effects of early training with the outcome of no training at all, and had the training been really lengthy and intensive, the differences in the twins' abilities might have been immense.

A deprivation experiment

At least in principle, an alternative way to discover to what extent differences in early experiences can accelerate or retard development would be to undertake long-term twin experiments in which one twin is given unusually intensive early training and the other twin is deprived of potentially valuable experiences. In practice, of course, there are ethical arguments against undertaking any investigation of this kind. For that reason it is widely assumed that no experimental study has been undertaken that involves deliberately depriving children of early experiences. But as it happens, that assumption is wrong.

An experimental study, undertaken in the 1930s, examined the effects of deliberately depriving infant girls (Dennis, 1941; Dennis and Dennis, 1951). Two baby girls, fraternal (non-identical) twins, were cared for from the age of one month until they were 14 months old in the home of a husband and wife team, the Dennises. The intention was to deprive both infants of any stimulation beyond what was necessary for essential physical care. They were fed, regularly changed, and kept warm, but no further care was given. The room in which they lived contained no toys, no pictures, and very little furniture. The Dennises tried to avoid rewarding or punishing the twins at all, and abstained from actions that could be readily imitated.

At first, the effects of depriving the children in these ways appeared to be fairly small. On a number of tests administered during their first seven months, the twins' scores were within the normal range for babies of comparable age, although they were backward on some items. But their subsequent development was more seriously retarded. According to nearly all the tests administered to measure their progress in later months, until the termination of the study when they were 14 months of age, the twins' progress was much below average. This outcome is especially impressive in view of the fact that the deprivation they suffered was by no means particularly severe. The twins were in fact given two hours of undivided attention each day by caring adults, which is more than many babies experience.

By demonstrating that deprivation can seriously retard children's early development, the findings obtained by the Dennises provide additional evidence of the powerful effects of a child's experiences on progress in the early years. The fact that the twins' performance levels later returned to normal, after they had received extra training following the termination of the main study, provides further evidence of the impact of early experiences.

Accelerating physical skills

Many studies of accelerated early learning have been, like the ones in which Gesell was involved, too brief in duration and insufficiently intensive to provide a reliable indication of the likely outcome of a truly massive intervention that greatly increases a child's opportunities for early learning. The findings of a more substantial intervention were reported by Myrtle McGraw (1935; 1939). Her subjects were fraternal twin boys. One of them (Johnny) was given training on five days each week between the ages of seven months and 24 months. A number of physical skills were taught. The other twin (Jimmy) received less than three months' training, and even this was delayed until he reached the age of 22 months. At that time he was given intensive tutition for a period of two and a half months, in the same activities on which Johnny had received earlier and more prolonged training.

The effects of the long-term early training were dramatic. In all the skills that Johnny was taught, he progressed well beyond the average levels of competence for boys of his age. He was also well ahead of his twin. For instance, by ten months he swam on his own, and he could dive from the side of a swimming-pool at 15 months and from a diving board at 17 months. Compared with his twin he was bolder and more self-confident, especially when faced with a new physical challenge. By this age he was also a moderately accomplished roller-skater, and could climb up steep slopes.

These findings show that, with appropriate training, a substantial degree of early acceleration can be achieved. Since the untrained twin did not make any unusual progress at any of the skills, it is possible to be reasonably sure that the accelerated learning was caused by the exceptional learning opportunities that were provided. But did the effects last? In order to find out, McGraw (1939) assessed the twins again when they were six years old. She found that Johnny, the twin who was trained early, was still well ahead of the other boy on all the complex skills that had been taught. He was much better at running, climbing, jumping, walking, swimming, and riding a tricycle. In physical tasks generally, he displayed greater muscular coordination and more daring. The other twin,

Jimmy, was more timid and much more awkward. Even at the age of 22 years, when some of the twins' motor skills were filmed, it was clear that the twin who had been given early training retained some important advantages. For example, when seen climbing a ladder, he was clearly more confident and enthusiastic than his twin and also more skilled.

Since McGraw's classic experiment, other researchers have conducted investigations designed to assess the effects of intensive early training on physical skills. Broadly speaking, their findings provide strong confirmation for those of McGraw. That is to say, well-planned interventions that are reasonably intensive and long-lasting reliably produce substantial early gains in children's abilities. For example, Fowler *et al.* (1983) found that over a period of 15 weeks in which four-year-olds received three 30-minute training sessions each week in gymnastic skills, the children made large improvements in their scores at tests measuring complex movement patterns that were similar to the skills that had been taught. Their gains were no less than five times as large as the progress achieved over the same 15-week period by children who had no special gymnastics training.

There were some limits to the effectiveness of these procedures, however. For example, the gains of the trained children on tests of simple motor abilities that were unrelated to the contents of the training programme were small, and not significantly greater than the improvements made over the same period by those children who were given no training in gymnastics. It appears that the advantages of early training may be restricted to the particular skills that are taught.

Accelerating the acquisition of language

One fairly common view among parents is that although it may be possible, with intensive early training, to accelerate the acquisition of some skills, the development of certain fundamental human abilities simply cannot be accelerated, and attempts to speed up the learning of them are simply a waste of time. Language is one such ability. Children do not seem to need to be taught language: they all learn to talk, even if the parents make no particular efforts to teach them. It has even been observed that deliberate teaching can impede language rather than accelerate it. A research team headed by Katherine Nelson discovered that children whose mothers rewarded them for pronouncing words correctly and punished them for poor pronunciation made less progress than children whose mothers were relatively unconcerned about correct pronunciation (Nelson *et al.*, 1973). And although numerous studies have found various aspects of child development to be strongly correlated with the child's experience of language, and particularly with the amount, form, and quality of language stimulation provided by the mother (Clarke-Stewart, 1973; Fowler, 1990) or by the staff in day care centres (McCartney, 1984), sceptics have been able to point out that since the evidence is only correlational it does not prove that differences in children's language experiences actually caused the differences between children in their language abilities. Chomsky and other theorists have put forward strong arguments for believing that human brains need to be innately wired up in particular ways in order for it to be possible for the young of our species to become competent at using language. One author went so far as to entitle his book on language 'The Language Instinct' (Pinker, 1994).

However, while it is true that language has some of the characteristics of an instinct, in other respects it is not like an instinct at all. In particular, it is unlike an instinct in that its acquisiton can be strongly affected by experience, as was evident from the findings of the study by Betty Hart and Todd Risley that was described at the beginning of Chapter 2. These researchers discovered that underlying the variations between children from diverging social classess in their language development, there were huge differences in the children's actual experiences of language.

A number of other studies have evaluated the effectiveness of efforts to accelerate language acquisition. These efforts have been surprisingly successful. The main outcome has been to show that, contradicting the assertions that have been made about the pointlessness of trying to encourage faster progress in language without waiting for physical maturation to take place, the linguistic development of babies can indeed be brought forward, and very considerably.

Most of the language acceleration studies have been relatively narrow in scope and of short duration, and based on infants who were no younger than around nine months of age. In contrast, an interesting set of small-scale experimental studies by William Fowler and his co-researchers (Fowler *et al.*, 1983; Fowler, 1990) examined the progress of 15 infants from the age of around five months. The babies were taught by their parents, in their own homes, and the parents received tuition and guidance from the investigators. The latter had devised a graduated language programme. This began with activities designed to teach single-word referents for objects and actions, and gently moved on to more advanced elements of language, including more complex parts of speech and various grammatical forms. Some of the families were from the middle class, and were at least moderately well educated, but other families had little formal education. For instance, there were some Italian-speaking parents in the study who were functionally illiterate.

Broadly speaking, the elements of language training in the programme were not very different from the kinds of activities that many parents spontaneously initiate, except that

1. they took place more regularly and frequently, and
2. involved a larger proportion of the time available;
3. they began when the baby was considerably younger than usual;
4. they were systematic, consistent, and more carefully graduated; and
5. more emphasis was placed on the recording, by the parents, of both the parental training procedures and the babies' early progress at understanding and using language.

Much of the language stimulation took place in the context of informal play activities and social interactions that the infants found pleasurable. Parents were encouraged to be consistent with their labelling of word items, to keep play activities simple enough to match their infants' capacities, and to devote time to play that involved social play ('peek-a-boo' for instance), and identifying physical objects and items shown in picture books and magazines. To help the parents, a training manual was distributed and its contents discussed with them. Lists of words were provided, and, for some poorly educated families, picture books.

In order to assess the effects of the programme, some other infants, of similar ages, were allocated to a control condition. These infants, like the ones who did receive training, were given language tests in their sixth month and again in their twelfth month, but unlike the others they did not receive special instruction in the intervening period.

The outcome was impressive, to say the least. After the six-month period the trained infants' language development was well ahead of the norms for babies of equivalent ages. For example, by their twelfth month four of the infants were speaking in sentences, an achievement that is not usually encountered until around the twentieth month. By 20 months, three of the infants were using five-word sentences. By 24 months, almost all were doing so, although the average age at which that level of language performance is reached is no less than 32 months. They began to use pronouns at 18 months on average (compared with the norm of 23 months), self-referral pronouns such as *I* and *me* at 18 months (compared with 29 months), and plurals before 24 months (compared with the 34-month norm). They first began to comprehend words between five and seven months, and they became able to speak four or more words between eight and 12 months, in both cases well ahead of the age norms. Quantitatively, over the course of the first six months' training they gained just under 40 points in language quotient test scores on the Griffiths language test, rising from an initial mean score of 101 (which indicates that at the time the study began, when they were in their sixth month of age, their scores, as a group, were broadly average for infants of that age) to a mean of 139, after six months' training – an exceptionally high score. In contrast, the scores of infants allocated to the control conditions, who did not receive special language training, were all around 100 or lower at the end of the six-month period. That is, they remained broadly average for infants of their age.

The long-term outcomes were equally striking. Those children whose parents continued to record their progress and engage in the kinds of language activities recommended in the programme, maintained, and sometimes increased, their superiority at using language, at least until they were five years old, at which time the final occasion on which they were tested occurred. The gains were fully maintained in most of those children who came from families in which language and language-related skills were emphasized and valued.

It is interesting to note that the only middle-class family in which the gains were not maintained was one in which, at the end of the initial six-month study, when the child was 12 months of age, the mother told the researchers that she was discontinuing further stimulation and intended to give only routine care in the future. Her reason was that she wanted to be sure that her boy would not be different from other children (Fowler *et al.*, 1983, p. 105). Her decision had devastating effects on the child's progress. Between the age of 12 months and 18 months (at which time the children were tested again) this child's language quotient score, in sharp contrast with the other children's, dropped from 168 to 134. His IQ score declined even more dramatically, from 149 to 118.

Fowler's findings demonstrate that intensive language stimulation in early infancy can have large and persisting positive effects. It is clear that appropriate stimulation and encouragement does lead to rapid increases in essential language skills. The six-month programme produced greatly accelerated language development in all the children who participated. Despite the relatively short duration of the intervention, the children's progress, by the end of it, was well ahead of the normal. They uttered their first words between two and six months in advance of the average child, their first sentences were produced three to eight months before the normal age, and their vocabularies at the age of 14 months were about ten months ahead of the established norms.

The results of another investigation show that even relatively brief language training can produce substantial and long-lasting advantages. In a study by Whitehurst *et al.* (1988), middle-class parents were taught to give their children more encouragement to talk, and better feedback, during the times when parents were reading to the children from picture books. The children's ages ranged from 21 months to 35 months.

The parents were trained to incorporate three principles in their interactions with their children. First, they were shown how to encourage children to talk about the contents of the pictures, rather than passively listening and looking. The parents were told to ask 'what?' questions (for example, 'There's Eeyore. What's happening to him?'; or 'Do you think that Kitty will get into trouble?'), designed to get the child to participate actively, rather than questions requiring only a 'yes' or 'no' answer, or ones that focused on names (for example, 'Who's that?'). Second, the parents were encouraged to be as informative as possible in the feedback they provided for their children. They were to expand on their children's answers or demonstrate alternative possibilities. Third, the parents were told to make progressive changes in the form of their interventions and their interactions with the child. For instance, parents were encouraged to make sure that a child knew the names of objects in a book before starting to introduce questions about the attributes and relationships of the characters which a book depicted.

The parents who participated in this study taped their home reading sessions with their children. That made it possible for the experimenters to measure the degree to which the planned intervention was actually implemented. The duration of the experimental intervention was only one month, but in order to measure its longer-term effects, the children were tested nine months afterwards, as well as at the end of the one-month period.

The interventions had marked positive effects on the children's use of language. Compared with subjects in a control group, the 30 trained children obtained scores at the end of the one-month training period that were eight months ahead on one test, the Illinois Test of Psycholinguistic Abilities, and six months ahead on another, The Expressive One-Word Picture Vocabulary Test. (On a third test, the Peabody Picture Vocabulary Test – Revised, they scored better than the control-group children, but the difference was not statistically significant.) Nine months later, the children in the experimental group were still six months ahead of the others in each of the first two language tests.

The authors of the study draw attention to the fact that this dramatic improvement occurred despite the fact that the programme was highly economical, requiring only one hour of direct training for the parents, and despite the fact that the children who formed the control group had conscientious and strongly motivated middle-class parents who read to them just as frequently as the parents of the children in the experimental group read to their children. These findings suggest that there is considerable scope for acceleration in most children's language development. As the authors point out,

> Many parents of normal young children spend hours per week reading to them and purchase hundreds of picture books to facilitate that activity. Our research demonstrates that the reading behavior of parents is not optimal, even within a highly select, motivated, affluent sample. The implication is that changes in parental behavior that are not particularly difficult to obtain could have substantial positive effects on children's language development. (Whitehurst *et al.*, 1988, p. 557)

The findings of other studies investigating the outcomes of language interventions are broadly similar to those obtained by Fowler's and Whitehurst's research teams. For instance, J. McVicker Hunt (1986) observed the effects of intensive special language stimulation by caregivers who had been trained in language acquisition techniques that placed stress on verbal interactions. The special training, which commenced when infants were just four weeks old, had large positive effects on the language development of children in a Teheran orphanage. These children progressed considerably faster than other children brought up in the conditions of the orphanage, and at the age of two years their language achievements were broadly equivalent to those of children brought up in professional families in the United States. In studies by Drash and Stolberg (cited by Fowler, 1983) training produced large gains in vocabulary and language use in a small sample of young children. Two-year-olds in another study made substantial gains in grammatical skills following instruction totalling no more than five hours in duration (Nelson, 1977). Hamilton (1977) and Metzl (1980) among others, observed similar improvements in early language skills in considerably younger children as a result of language stimulation. Whitehurst and Valdez-Menchaca (1988) observed that reinforcing children aged two and three years (by complying with their requests for toys) for saying words in a foreign language produced major increases and improvements in language use.

Other researchers have noticed similar improvements in language skills following appropriate social or material rewards in normal infants as young as six months (Staats, 1971) and in older mentally handicapped children (Guess, 1969; Guess and Baer, 1973). The latter findings, added to previous evidence that aspects of children's language are correlated to the responsiveness of mothers to children's utterances (Petersen and Sherrod, 1982) and that mothers react differently to their children's word and non-word responses, show that reinforcement is not at all unimportant in children's first-language acquisition.

What seems to be especially crucial is not the sheer amount of speech that is directed towards the child, but its appropriateness. For example, adult labelling of objects is more likely to result in the child learning the objects' names when the child is already expressing an interest in them than when the mother has to draw the child's attention to the objects (White, 1985; Valdez-Menchaca and Whitehurst, 1988; Hart and Risley, 1990). Research by Paula Menyuk and others has shown that it is extremely important for adults to talk to infants and young children, rather than at them. Many parents, without being of aware of it, are inclined to do the latter. It is particularly important for an adult who has made a comment or asked a question to pause and give the baby some time to respond. Parents often find it difficult to do this. Even if the infant is too young to make a verbal response, it is helpful to communicate an understanding of the concept of a conversation or dialogue, in which each partner takes turns in attending to the other person and in taking a more active role. It is hardly surprising that the kind of 'incidental' language teaching that is most effective is only likely to occur when an adult and a child are together in a one-to-one situation. Only in these circumstances can the adult be in a position to know what is currently engaging the child's attention.

Taken together, the research findings provide conclusive evidence that young children's language skills can be substantially accelerated, to the extent that it would be commonplace for an observer to regard the child's linguistic development as being exceptional. In other words, 'serious attention to the quality of cognitively oriented language stimulation from infancy will enable virtually all children enjoying salutary home environments to surpass cultural norms for language development, often reaching levels historically associated with "giftedness" ' (Fowler, 1990).

Does language acceleration matter? Is it worth the effort? Both these questions justify a strongly positive answer because gaining language fundamentally transforms a child's mental capabilities. Because our thinking is so thoroughly infused with and controlled by language, we find it hard even to envision mental life in its absence. It is almost impossible for a person whose thought patterns are based on language to conceive of the ways in which life is experienced by an individual who lacks language. Words such as accelerating, augmenting, increasing, extending, or magnifying fail to do justice to the real nature of the transformation that takes place as a result of linguistic abilities being acquired. They open up, irreversibly, new and previously inconceivable patterns of thinking. Consequently, a one-year-old who acquires key language skills several months earlier than is usual will be gaining enormous advantages over other children. Parents who take steps to increase their infant's early opportunities to learn language skills can be confident that their efforts will be rewarded.

Early reading

Large numbers of children learn to read early, well before they start attending a school where reading is formally taught. It is difficult to ascertain just how many young children read and how early, because there is no one agreed criterion by which a child can be judged to have learned to read. Reading encompasses a large number of separate sub-skills. (The fact that failure at just one of them can hamper the child's all-round performance as a reader is one of the reasons for so many children experiencing difficulty in reading.) Consequently, it is not possible to state a precise age at which a child has mastered reading, just as it is not possible to say exactly when a person has learned to play the piano. There are, of course, a number of tests designed to measure a child's progress in reading, but comparisons are often difficult because different studies of early reading have tended to use different tests.

Reading is one area of competence in which the advantages of accelerated learning for many children are likely to be considerable, and perhaps more so than people generally realize. Some of the outcomes for a child of gaining particular capabilities deserve attention. Everybody agrees that being able to read is an invaluable ability, and one that is essential for the enjoyment of a full life in a literate culture. Everybody assents to the view that reading provides access to many kinds of information and knowledge, and opens up areas of experience and insight and understanding that are closed to the non-reader. It is universally acknowledged that the skill of reading, if properly exploited, can extend and amplify the intellectual grasp of any human learner (Olson, 1977, 1986; Kress, 1982). It is obvious that reading empowers people by giving them a capacity to learn independently that is denied to non-readers.

Yet the actual impact on a young person of learning to read is often underestimated. Because we have been able to read for as long as we can remember, we may fail to realize that certain very basic kinds of knowledge about language, which we tend to assume are available to all language users, are in fact the products of literacy, and outside the grasp of illiterate people. For instance, even the concept of a word can have no very precise meaning to anyone who cannot read. Asking an illiterate child or adult to recite a poem word for word or line by line is asking that person to do something that is impossible because it has no clear meaning for them. Similarly, the idea of the 'correct' form of a poem being embodied in a text only makes sense to people in a literate community. Consequently, when people from oral cultures are asked to attempt verbatim reproduction of a song or a passage of poetry, their degree of success, as measured in terms of word to word agreement with a previous version, may be sharply restricted (Ong, 1982).

Literate people tend to assume that the flow of heard language divides itself naturally into words, but it actually does no such thing. Examination of a speech spectrogram – essentially a visual record of the sound of a language sequence – reveals no reliable information specifying where one word ends and the next begins. That information is not made explicit in the flow of language, as is easily verified by listening to a sample of speech in an unfamiliar foreign language. It is necessary to be a reader in order to have a really good understanding of the manner in which language is structured. Without literacy, language exists only as sound, and it is difficult for a non-reader to conceive of the possibility that there exists a body of stored knowledge that can be looked up. All thinking will bear the marks of this limitation. For instance, where writing does not exist, the necessity to ensure that what has been thought can later be recalled forces the individual to adopt a number of devices specifically designed to facilitate the accurate retention and retrieval of the information. In oral cultures, such devices may involve the use of highly rhymed or rhythmic language, the introduction of balanced language patterns, repetitions, antitheses, assonances, alliterations, and the use of standard, well-remembered language formulas that are easily recalled simply because they are highly familiar. Within a purely oral and non-literate culture it is very difficult to have the kinds of thoughts that we would describe as being abstract or original.

Of course, the experience of a non-literate child living in a literate culture is not the same as that of a person in an oral culture. But they both encounter similar limitations on thinking and understanding. Until a child learns to read, that individual is not simply denied access to the resources of information and knowledge that literacy makes available, but may have limited awareness of the very idea of accessible stored knowledge. The non-reader is not just unable to do certain intellectual tasks that depend on having access to information, but is also to a large extent quite unable to grasp what he or she is missing.

Accelerated learning aside, there is considerable evidence that the likelihood of a child making even normal progress towards learning to read at school will be impeded if certain skills have not been gained before the beginning of formal instruction. One group of basic skills that appear to be necessary for learning to read involves the ability to be aware of the smallest sound units of language, *phonemes*. A child who does not perceive phonemes accurately or is unable to discriminate between two different phonemes (such as the *b* in *bad* and the *d* in *dad*) will almost certainly find it very difficult to learn to read (Bryant and Bradley, 1985; Coles, 1987). Bradley and Bryant (1983) asked four- and five-year-olds to listen to lists of around three words, in which in every word but one there was a common phoneme. The child's task was to say which was the odd word. The researchers found that the children's performance level at this task was a good predictor of the same children's achievements at reading and spelling four years later.

This finding shows that there is some connection between phonological skills in early childhood and subsequent progress at learning to read. But does it follow that differences in phonological skills are a cause of variability in children's reading achievements? To investigate that, Bradley and Bryant selected 65 children who did poorly at the above phoneme discrimination task, and who therefore would have been considered 'at risk', so far as success at reading was concerned. These children were divided into four groups. The first two groups were given training in categorizing sounds. The training was not particularly time-consuming or intensive: each child was seen for twenty 10-minute sessions per year, for two years. Group 1 children were taught to discriminate between phoneme sounds and those in Group 2 were given the same instruction but were also taught to associate letter sounds with actual letters. The children in Group 3 were taught to discriminate between categories, but their training did not include discriminating between sounds, and Group 4 children received no instruction at all.

The children in all four groups were tested when they had reached the age of eight years. By this time Group 4 children, who had not been given any special training, were lagging a year behind the normal standard of achievement at reading, and at spelling they were two whole years behind the average. Group 3 children, who had received training at making discriminations, but not ones that involved phonemes, were also below average at both the reading and spelling tests. Both of the groups who had been given training at discriminating between phonemes were doing considerably better. The Group 1 children were nevertheless slightly below average at reading, and worse at spelling, but the children who had been in Group 2, and who had been trained to discriminate between phonemes and to make associations between sounds and letters, were successfully reading at the level that was expected for children of their age.

Other studies have confirmed that preschool instruction in basic skills involving letters, sounds, and phonemes can lead to big improvements in a child's progress in reading at school and can considerably reduce the likelihood of a child experiencing difficulties in learning to read. For instance, in one study it was found that training young children to blend sounds together, and to break words down into their constituent sounds, produced substantial gains in early reading (Goldstein, 1976). It is possible that many of the problems that lead to a child being diagnosed as having 'learning disabilities' or as being dyslexic have their roots in a failure on the part of adults to appreciate that the child lacks certain fundamental skills that are necessary. Coles (1987) has suggested that many problems arise from teachers wrongly assuming that all children entering school already possess certain basic or 'prerequisite' skills that reading depends upon. Children may fail to make progress due to a lack of fundamental skills that may not be taught in school because of the erroneous assumption that they have already gained them.

It would be wrong to infer that all parents must provide formal training in either phonological skills or the other abilities that are necessary in order for a child to be able to learn to read. Parents who regularly read to their children, and encourage children to enjoy the kinds of rhyming and other language games that are commonplace in homes in which written materials are regularly used, usually find that children gain the required prerequisite skills in the absence of specific or formal instruction.

When a young child has learned to read earlier than most, before going to school, a close examination of the circumstances almost always reveals that the child has received considerable assistance from an adult or an older child who has been prepared to spend a good deal of time working with the young learner. The vast majority of children who learn to read early are taught, usually in a fairly informal manner, by their parents. Although it is not uncommon for a biographical or autobiographical account to state that a particular child taught herself (or himself) to read, the fact of the matter is that this simply cannot be done. No child (and no adult, either) can learn to read entirely on his or her own. A certain amount of help is essential. There must be someone to draw the child's attention to the particular features and associations that reading draws upon. Tribespeople in isolated villages where no-one can read do not become literate, if only because there is nobody to teach them the skill.

Can any normal child learn to read considerably earlier than the usual age? Knowing that many children do learn to read while they are still very young provides a reason for believing that, in principle, the correct answer may be a positive one. In practice, however, many young children will not only lack necessary language skills but may have failed to gain the mental skills that enable a person to concentrate on learning tasks. Young children are often too impulsive and too easily distracted to be able to sustain the concentration that reading skills demand. In reality, whether or not the a child does learn to read early will largely depend on the extent to which the indvidual's experiences have given the child the kinds of motivations, interests, and curiosity that makes a young person *want* to read. Having opportunities to gain the desire to read is just as important as having access to the necessary guidance and tuition. As one might expect, there is firm evidence that children's progress at reading is related to the quality and the quantity of reading experiences at home (Moon and Wells, 1979): there is no better predictor of a child's reading achievement.

As early as 1931, Helen Davidson published the findings of a study designed to assess the effects of providing special training in reading to various children, including a group of five bright three-year-olds (Davidson, 1931). Each child had a daily ten-minute individual reading lesson, five days per week, over a four-month period. Davidson reports that on each day there was also a brief group game, based on reading skills, lasting for about five minutes per day. Various reading tests were administered before the programme and at the end of it, and also several months afterwards.

The maximum amount of individual instruction received over the total period was no more than just over six hours. Nevertheless, all five of the three-year-olds made substantial progress. For example, at the end of the study each of them could recognize, on average, 129 words that were shown to them out of context. All gained reading skills equal to those usually found in children about two years older. Two of the five displayed reading ability equivalent to that of an average seven-year-old who had completed a year's formal schooling, and one was reading as well as a normal eight-year-old.

The findings of a project carried out by Arthur Staats (1971) provide some useful evidence concerning the possibility of children who do poorly in intelligence tests learning to read unusually early. Staats regarded his project primarily as a test of the effectiveness of certain behaviour modification procedures that were built into his course of instruction. These involved rewarding subjects with tokens that could be exchanged later for a variety of desirable prizes. The length of the instructional sessions totalled around 17 hours, made up of a large number of short trials lasting between five and eight minutes. One subject was a four-year-old boy with an IQ of 89. By the end of the programme he had acquired reading and writing skills that were advanced for his age, despite his low IQ and in spite of the fact that he came from a culturally deprived home environment. Staats draws attention to the finding that when the same training procedure was followed with another child with a much higher IQ, of 130, the rate of progress was not noticeably faster. For Staats, the similar achievements despite the large IQ differences demonstrate that with appropriate teaching most children learn quickly (Staats, 1971, p. 112).

These results seem to contradict the common view that a high IQ may be necessary for early reading. The number of participants in Staats' study was very small, but some results obtained by Durkin (1966), with a larger sample of subjects, provide further evidence that although progress at reading and IQ level tend to be related, reading level does not necessarily depend on a child's level of intelligence. Durkin found that, even when children reached the age of 11, the reading skills of children who had learned to read at three years remained two years in advance of children who learned to read when they were five despite the fact that the two groups did not differ in their IQ scores.

In conclusion, it appears that at least the majority of children are capable of learning to read at least a year or two earlier than the age when this is usually achieved. As well as the findings I have described, additional evidence surveyed by Fowler (1983) supports this view. And it is generally found that early advantages in reading are maintained for at least several years.

Of course, the fact that early reading is possible does not mean that it is always desirable. The possibility has been raised that early reading could have negative effects on a child. In fact, adverse effects were not seen in any of the studies that compared early readers with other children (Durkin, 1966), and the findings point to a number of positive outcomes. For instance, Scott and Bryant (cited by Fowler, 1983) found that early readers were more independent than other children, played with their peers just as frequently, were more purposive, and interacted more often with adults. However, correlational evidence of this kind can never be entirely conclusive concerning causes and effects. It is quite possible that reading makes children more independent, but it is equally possible that independent children are more likely to read early than others, or that other factors encourage them both to be independent and to learn to read.

Accelerating progress at musical skills

The evidence concerning the effectiveness of attempts to accelerate young children's progress is somewhat sketchy. Not nearly enough of it has taken the form of experimental studies in which fair-sized samples of children who have had special teaching are compared with otherwise similar children who have not received any exceptional treatment. But, such as they are, the available research findings are definitely consistent with the view that the majority of children are capable of acquiring most skills considerably earlier than is usual. As well as movement-based skills, language and reasoning, a variety of other abilities have been found to be amenable to acceleration in young children. These include a number of mathematical skills, memory skills, and abilities underlying Piagetian concepts such as conservation and seriation.

There have been a number of experimental studies of the effects of early training in the realm of music. Generally speaking, attempts to teach musical skills to young children are successful (Shuter-Dyson & Gabriel, 1981), although the outcomes tend to be specific to the particular abilities that are taught. Moreover, skills acquired unusually early are much more likely to be maintained if the school or home environment provides opportunities to practise them. By the age of six months, infants who receive extensive opportunities to practise (over a 40-day period) can learn to match musical pitches that are produced on a pipe. However, infants aged less than one year do not appear to be capable of imitating melodies (Sloboda, 1985), although, according to Shuter-Dyson and Gabriel (1981), a small-scale study by McFie was effective in teaching the investigator's 15-month-old son to sing the first four bars of the theme of the Andante of Haydn's Surprise Symphony. Early research by Jersild and Bienstock (1931) established that children as young as two years of age can greatly benefit from instruction in singing, and that early advantages may be maintained for some years.

Young children also profit from aural training that is designed to help them to discriminate between notes. They can learn to recognize musical items even when they are played on new instruments (Fullard, 1967). Shuter-Dyson and Gabriel describe an interesting study by Kukenski, in which folk tunes were played to infants between the ages of three and nine months. During the training sessions a song, lasting 30 seconds, would be repeated ten times, accompanied by a puppet which moved in synchrony. There were also a number of accompanying exercises, designed to encourage the babies to move rhythmically and respond to the tune. Subsequent tests showed that the training had been effective in accelerating the infants' musical responsiveness. Those infants who had been given training over a six-month period performed significantly better than children who only had three months of musical enrichment, and the latter children did better than babies in a control group who received no special musical training at all. As in the case of other abilities, differences in experience lead to differences in coding strategies between children who have had musical training and untrained individuals (Dowling, 1988) and corresponding differences in the ways in which they represent music and communicate musical expressions (Bamberger, 1986; Davidson and Scripp, 1988).

The successes of young children who have been exposed to the Suzuki method of musical training demonstrate that far more preschoolers are capable of gaining impressive instrumental skills than anyone would have predicted a generation ago. There has been little systematic research into the consequences and limitations of the kinds of musical training provided by the Suzuki method, but the achievements of numerous young children who have followed Suzuki procedures prove that in the right circumstances many children, and perhaps most, are indeed capable of impressive musical accomplishments. The successes of the Suzuki programme are not unrelated to its child-centred and carefully graduated nature, and its emphasis on engaging the child's interest and motivation, and that of the parent as well. In the early stages much emphasis is placed on developing a proper attitude to the learning task, and the children are required to reaffirm their commitment to the training by respectfully requesting instruction at the beginning of each session. At an early stage they begin to establish a habit of concentrated daily practice, and they are taught a number of routines that are painstakingly practised until they become an automatic and smoothly executed part of the lessons (Peak, 1986; Taniuchi, 1986). William Fowler notes that over a period of years the child gradually gains concepts of musical language and an understanding of pitch, rhythm, tempo, and other musical concepts, just as the infant becomes familiar with the ordinary dimensions of language.

My own research, conducted in cooperation with John Sloboda and Jane Davidson (Sloboda & Howe, 1991; Howe *et al.*, 1995) has shown that young children are capable of making substantial progress towards mastery of a musical instrument, but only when they can count on considerable adult support. They benefit considerably from having a teacher who can succeed in establishing good relationships with young learners, and who can help motivate the child to do well as well as building up self-confidence and helping the child to become enthusiastic about playing music. Children also benefit from supportive parents.

It is especially helpful for parents to provide assistance and encouragement in relating to practising. There is a reason for that. On the one hand, it is necessary to practise regularly and frequently in order to make progress, as we discovered in Chapter 1. On the other hand, repeated practising is not inherently motivating for most young children. It requires attention, it tends to be a solitary activity, and involves considerable repetition. In other words, as was also seen in Chapter 2, it is not the kind of activity that most young people enjoy, even at adolescence. Consequently, in order to ensure that young children practise sufficiently to make good progress, they will need plenty of help and encouragement. It is the parents who are in the best position to provide this, by giving a child company when practising, by offering plenty of praise and encouragement, and by adding to the enjoyability of practising, by making practice activities into games.

The parents of those children who make the most progress often help them in other ways. These parents tend to have close contacts with the music teacher, thereby keeping in touch with the child's progress and becoming well-informed about ways to help. Often, although not always, these parents will have musical interests themselves, and music will be a familiar element of the home background. Gradually, a child who practises regularly will acquire a habit of practising and, as we have seen in Chapter 2, this makes it easier to get on with the task. For the child, musical training becomes a regular and important part of daily life, and when that happens steady progress is likely.

Extraordinary skills in ordinary adults

Studies investigating the possibility of accelerating the progress of young children form one way, but not the only way, to discover whether or not someone has to be to be inherently extraordinary in order to gain exceptional abilities. An alternative approach to this question is to examine the possibility of 'ordinary' adult people acquiring skills that are extraordinary, to the extent that it is customarily assumed that they demand innately exceptional capabilities. If it is found to be possible for individuals who, at the beginning of training, have no special abilities or talents to gain a particular skill that has been regarded as impossible to acquire in the absence of appropriate inborn qualities, the case for the necessity of such qualities would be seriously weakened. And if it is also discovered that each of a variety of different skills that have been regarded as depending upon the existence of inborn talents can be gained by people who lack any special innate qualities, it would seem appropriate to question the assumption that there exist any mental abilities that can only be acquired by individuals who have been endowed from birth with certain unusual qualities.

There have been a number of reports of people having an exceptional ability to remember. (A particularly fascinating example is the well-known case study by Luria (1968) of a Russian journalist whose memory for information was so accurate and reliable that he was able to make a living by performing memory feats on the stage.) It has generally been assumed that the memory systems of such individuals must have been fundamentally exceptional from the time of birth. Obviously, such a deduction would be called into question if it were found that their feats were equalled or excelled by ordinary people who, at the start of a period of training, displayed no remarkable ability to remember. As it happens, some investigations by Anders Ericsson and others have demonstrated that with appropriate training ordinary individuals are indeed capable of gaining abilities that are remarkably superior to normal levels of achievement.

In one study, which was briefly mentioned earlier, in Chapter 2, Chase and Ericsson (1981) trained a young adult male at a memory feat over a period of more than two years. He was paid to practise for one hour per day at a simple memory task that involved listening to, and then immediately attempting to repeat, lists containing random digits presented at a rate of one item per second. The largest number of randomly ordered digits that most people can recall without error in these conditions is around eight or nine items. Practising the task for up to ten hours or so produces only a small improvement. And because a small amount of practice does not substantially increase the memory span, it has traditionally been assumed that no amount of practice will produce a large improvement (Howe, 1980, 1983, 1984, 1988d). As a result, it was widely agreed that everyone has an essentially unchangeable 'memory span', limited to around eight items, for unrelated verbal items such as digits, letters, or words.

What was new about the approach of Chase and Ericsson was that these researchers questioned the above assumptions. Instead of giving just ten or so hours of practice, like the earlier investigators, they paid their subject to practise for closer to 1000 hours. This had dramatic consequences. After two years, the individual's memory span increased to around 80 items, roughly ten times the length of span that had long been regarded as being essentially fixed, and impossible to increase. Without going into details about how the massive increase was achieved, it is enough to say that that particular individual gradually acquired strategies that made it possible for him to group a number of single digits together into larger multi-digit units that could be regarded as being (in many instances) running times for various athletic competitions. For this particular subject, these sequences of digits were meaningful, and therefore memorable, because they could be connected to his existing knowledge about one of his main interests, athletics. Another person might have evolved a strategy based on grouping items in different ways, ones that had meanings that were related to that individual's particular interests.

Similar improvements in memory span have been reported in a number of ordinary people. One person is described by Ericsson and Faivre (1988) as having achieved a memory span of over a hundred items, which at the time of writing was said to be still increasing. Ericsson and Faivre describe a number of additional studies which demonstrate that a variety of different memory skills are equally amenable to training. These researchers found that, after training, the participants were remarkably similar to individuals who had been described in case histories as having inherently exceptional memory abilities. In fact, it now seems likely that many of the feats of memory that are displayed by people who are said to have had an innately exceptional memory can be excelled by ordinary people.

It is important to be clear about precisely what is being trained in these studies. Practice does not produce a better memory. What it does succeed in doing is to give a person improved memory skills. These skills can be remarkably specific: typically they do not generalize or transfer to any extent to tasks that are different from the one that was practised. Consequently, for example, the individual who achieved a memory span of 80 items in Chase and Ericsson's investigation, remained no better than average at other kinds of memory tasks, despite all the training he had been given. It is true that some people who are reported as having an exceptionally good memory may perform extraordinarily well at each of a range of different kinds of memory tasks. But that is because they have been able to acquire a number of memory skills, not because they have 'a good memory'.

So rather than thinking of a person as having a good (or bad) memory, it is more realistic to think in terms of individuals possessing a number of relatively specific memory skills (Ericsson and Crutcher, 1988; Ericsson and Faivre, 1988). If people are given a battery of memory tests, the correlation between an individual's performance at the different tasks is usually near zero (Ericsson, 1985; Howe, 1989). In other words, the chances are that someone who is unusually successful at one test of memory will be no better than average at remembering something else. The commonsense view that there exist broad differences between people in their ability to retain all kinds of information in memory is largely incorrect.

People are good at remembering information which they are interested in and knowledgeable about, and poor at remembering those things which do not interest them. For example, research has shown that many British soccer enthusiasts can recall lengthy lists of match scores with impressive accuracy. Recall of soccer scores is highly correlated ($r = .8$) with knowledgeability about soccer, and unrelated to ability to remember other kinds of lists (Morris *et al.*, 1981; Morris *et al.*, 1985; Morris, 1988).

Many football enthusiasts can recall the scores of all 80-odd major weekend British soccer matches. How is that possible? The main reason is that whereas for someone who is uninterested in the sport a listing of football scores is no more than a list

of isolated random digits, for a knowledgeable football enthus-
iast that same list has many kinds of meanings and implications.
Every score is significant, and therefore interesting.

Similarly, someone who is an expert at the game of chess can
remember the positions of chess pieces on the board far more
accurately than a non-expert. It is not just a matter of being
familiar with the individual pieces. Were that the case, chess
experts would remember positions more accurately than other
people even when chess pieces are placed at random positions
on the board. In fact, they only do better when the pieces form
legitimate chess positions, indicating that it is the experts'
structured knowledge of the game of chess that enables them to
remember so well.

Unusual perceptual capabilities

There are certain perceptual skills which, because they are
genuinely 'exceptional' in the sense that very few people can
do them, may appear to depend upon the performer having
inherently special qualities. But as in the case of other kinds of
expertise, investigations have demonstrated that such skills
can in fact be acquired by any ordinary person who is prepared
to put in enough practice.

Sometimes the very rarity of unusual skills misleads people
into believing that, for ordinary individuals, they must be
impossible to acquire. But as Anders Ericsson has demonstrated, given sufficient time and patience, many adults are
able to gain perceptual skills that are remarkable enough to
have been cited in the past as being evidence that the person
seen doing them must have had special innate aptitudes
(Ericsson, 1985; Ericsson and Faivre, 1988). For instance, there
are a number of perceptual abilities which, because they are
rare, have traditionally been assumed necessitating the posses-
sion of special gifts or talents. However, that assumption has
been shown to be wrong when it has later been observed that
virtually anyone who receives appropriate training is capable
of gaining the skill in question. One study, for example,
revealed that the very unusual skill of being able to determine
the sex of chickens can be gained without inordinate difficulty,

provided that sufficient training and practice is given (Bieder-man and Shiffrar, 1987). So, too, can other uncommon percep-tual skills such as the ones underlying X-ray diagnosis, identifying heart murmurs, and wine-tasting. (Lave, 1988; Saxe, 1988). Perfect (absolute) pitch perception is another unusual ability which, because it is unusual, is often thought to be innate. But that too is an acquired skill, although it is undoubtedly very difficult to learn unless it is gained in early childhood (Brady, 1970; Costall, 1985; Sloboda, 1985).

Yet another rare ability is the capacity to make absolute judgements of colour hues. Perhaps surprisingly, a typical adult can identify only five of a set of 21 colours that are only slightly different. But with extended practice, performance improves very substantially. Following 80 training sessions, an individual studied by Ericsson and Faivre (1988) increased the number of similar hues he could correctly identify from 5 to 18 of the 21 differently coloured stimuli. Again, however, as in the case of memory training, the abilities acquired are highly specific ones. People acquire particular perceptual skills, not a generalized ability to make perceptual judgements or discriminations.

Some conclusions

Taken together, the findings that have been described in this chapter provide a strong case for arguing that, in principle, almost any person of normal intelligence may be capable of gaining impressive capabilities. In practice, there are numer-ous factors that prevent the majority of individuals from achieving the highest levels of success at difficult skills. Acquiring exceptional capabilities often demands enormous investments of time and concentration, unusual single-mind-edness, and exceptionally strong and sustained motivation. In reality, the necessarily very high degree of motivation and commitment is only likely to be encountered in a small number of people.

Yet there is an important distinction to be made between what someone is unlikely to achieve and what the person simply *cannot* achieve. Taken as a whole, the evidence provides virtually no support at all for the widely held view that very high levels of achievement are only possible for a few lucky individuals who have been singled out from birth to be the recipient of special gifts, talents, or aptitudes.

Possible negative consequences of accelerated learning

Until now, the desirability of attempting to accelerate the acquisiton of abilities by young people has not been seriously questioned. There are, of course, a number of matters that may cause concern, especially in connection with training activities that involve young children. There are certainly advantages for a child in having the kind of good start in life that can result from acquiring certain abilities unusually early, but these advantages have to be balanced against a number of possible disadvantages.

For a start, the pressures and high expectations that over-demanding parents may impose on a child can create serious problems. Also, there may be emotional costs resulting from an unusually specialized way of life during childhood. For instance, if the range of interests parents encourage is some-what narrow, there may be few opportunities for a young person to experience some of the activities of a normal childhood. It is quite possible for a childhood regime that is unusu-ally enriched, so far as opportunities to gain exceptional intellectual skills is concerned, to be at the same time one in which there is severe deprivation of other experiences that may be equally important ingredients of healthy development, even if they do not have obvious educational functions. So a child who does not have opportunities to play with other chil-dren may fail to gain shared interests and make friends, and consequently never acquire important social skills that people depend upon. Such a child will be at a serious disadvantage, even if he or she does gain intellectual capabilities at an unusually early age.

It is important to ensure that accelerating a child's early progress will bring real advantages to the individual concerned, and that those advantages will outweigh any likely disadvan-tages. What are the benefits for a child of acquiring particular abilities some months earlier than other children do? How are children directly affected by the intellectual skills they acquire? Up to a point, the answers to questions like these may be fairly obvious. Children make better than average progress towards gaining various kinds of valued abilities, and such progress helps to open the door to achievements that depend on those abilities. Other things being equal, the greater the early progress, the higher the probability of various peaks of achievement eventually being surmounted.

Chapter 4

Child prodigies

Accounts of the lives of child prodigies offer a useful source of insights into the circumstances in which a few children develop into the kinds of adults who are capable of impressive achievements. The evidence helps answer some questions concerning the causes of exceptionality, and raises further queries. This chapter begins by describing the early lives of two child prodigies, with the aim of conveying something of the manner in which progress is made by particular individual children. The two individuals whose childhoods I discuss are an English engineer, George Parker Bidder, and an American mathematician, Norbert Wiener.

Two prodigies: 1. George Bidder

George Parker Bidder was born in 1806 (coincidentally, within a month of the birth of John Stuart Mill, the best known of all child prodigies). He was the third son of a stonemason. At the age of six, with the encouragement of his older brother, another mason, George became interested in mental arithmetic. In his own words,

> there resided, in a house opposite to my father's, an aged blacksmith, a kind old man... on winter evenings I was allowed to perch myself on his forge hearth, listening to his stories. On one of these occasions, somebody by chance mentioned a sum;... I gave the answer correctly. This occasioned some little astonishment; they then asked me other questions, which I answered with equal facility... this increased my fame still more, and...

caused halfpence to flow into my pocket;... attaching me still more to the science of arithmetic. (Clark, 1983, pp. 3–4)

By the time George was nine his fame had spread enormously. He had already acquired a national reputation for his skill at mental calculations, and became known throughout England as 'The Calculating Boy'. He was exhibited up and down the country. A handbill advertising a forthcoming demonstration in Oxford when he was ten boasts that at a previous audience with 'her Majesty [Queen Charlotte, the wife of King George the Third] and the Dukes of Kent and Sussex, Earl Stanhope, Sir Joseph Banks, the Lord Mayor of London, and many other persons of the first distinction in the Kingdom' he had responded to the Duke of Kent's request to multiply 7953 by 4648 with the correct answer, 36 965 544. To the Queen's question, 'How many days would a Snail be creeping, at the rate of 8 feet per day, from the Land's End, in Cornwall, to Ferret's Head, in Scotland, the distance by admeasurement being 838 miles?', he again answered correctly, 553 080. Bidder was fast as well as accurate, although even he needed 13 minutes to do the largest of the mental calculation problems he was asked to solve, such as multiplying 257 689 435 by 356 875 649.

George Bidder was unquestionably a child prodigy, a term defined by another ex-prodigy as 'a child who has achieved an appreciable measure of adult intellectual standing before he is out of the years usually devoted to a secondary school education'. As a young child, the only formal education he received was at a small local school where only the most elementary arithmetic would have been taught. At the time he started to become extraordinarily adept at mental arithmetic he had not learned to read and write. Strangely enough, his lack of formal education was in some respects a blessing so far as his career as a boy prodigy was concerned, because a child who had learned mathematics at school would not have hit upon the methods that made it possible for George Bidder to do lengthy mental calculations. These methods are very different from the techniques that are most effective when written calculations are being done. As Bidder himself explained, with mental arithmetic, unlike arithmetic that involves using pencil and paper to retain the outcomes of various steps in a calculation, it is very important to keep the amount of information to be stored (in memory) at any one time to an absolute minimum. So with a calculation like 279 x 373 (to use his own example), he would start by multiplying 200 x 300 (= 60 000), to which he would add 200 x 70 (= 14 000), making 74 000 in all. To that total he would then add, successively, 200 x 3600, then 70 x 300 (= 21 000), 70 x 70 (= 4900), 70 x 3210), 9 x 300 (= 2700), 9 x 70 (= 630) and, finally, 9 x 3 (= 27), to give a grand total of 104 067.

This technique may look rather clumsy, compared with the methods of multiplication that are taught in school. But for anyone who is doing calculations mentally, it has the huge advantage of greatly reducing the load of data that has to be stored in memory while the computation is proceeding. All that needs to be remembered is one running total. With the written methods by which children are taught to do long multiplications at school it would be virtually impossible for anyone to do a problem such as this one mentally, without having access to pencil and paper for storing data. That is because the demands for retaining in memory the results of the intermediate steps in calculating would exceed what is humanly possible.

As well as providing a useful income, the exhibitions at which the young George Bidder was paraded as an infant prodigy up and down the country (about 50 years after Mozart had given his more renowned childhood performances) brought him to the attention of people who were willing to pay for him to receive a far better education in mathematics and other school subjects than would normally have been available to the child of an artisan family in rural England. When George was about nine, a group of distinguished scholars at Cambridge University examined him and arranged for him to be sent at their expense to Wilson's Grammar School, in Camberwell, near London. By the time he was 13 it had been arranged by a benefactor in the person of a wealthy Scottish lawyer, Henry Jardine, for George to receive private tutoring that would prepare him for entry to Edinburgh University. In those days it was not altogether uncommon for a wealthy individual to pay the costs of educating unusually promising youngsters. John Stuart Mill's father, James Mill, had profited from a similar arrangement. Like Bidder, James Mill attended Edinburgh University (Howe, 1998).

George Bidder entered that university in 1820 at the age of 14. (At the time this was not unusually young.) He stayed there for five successful years, during which he made a close friendship with a man who was to be very important in his subsequent career, the engineer Robert Stephenson, son of the railway pioneer George Stephenson (who, like Bidder, came from an impoverished background). Bidder's subsequent career as an engineer was remarkably busy and successful. His engineering achievements include numerous railways (among them the first railway to be built in the difficult terrain of Norway), large docks (including London's Victoria Docks, constructed on marshland in the Thames estuary), ships, bridges, aqueducts, viaducts, and a number of other large-scale projects including sewerage and water purification systems and telegraph communications works. With the Stephensons and Brunel, he was one of the great engineers of an age in which engineering was transforming many parts of the world. On Robert Stephenson's death he followed his friend as President of the Institution of Civil Engineers. Bidder died in 1878.

George Bidder was a genuine child prodigy. As we have seen, he was performing calculating feats at the age of seven that astounded spectators at local county fairs, and a year or two later he was able to solve problems that were beyond the powers of any living adult. At that time, of course, the ability to do difficult calculations in one's head had a real utility. His early efforts were powerfully rewarded: in all probability the exhibitions that were organized for him were at first designed simply to make a few shillings for his needy rural family. But as things turned out they did far more than that. As a result of the attention his early achievements attracted, new and previously unthinkable opportunities opened up for him. All kinds of future triumphs were made possible by the fact that he was able to draw to himself the attention of wealthy individuals who were prepared to finance a formal education at school and university. This would otherwise have been entirely outside the aspirations, let alone the means, of a person from his background.

2. Norbert Wiener

George Bidder's life highlights the extraordinariness of the feats that certain child prodigies have been capable of, and illustrates the possible consequences of a child's displaying exceptional mental skills at an early age. It would be pleasant to think that George Bidder's case provides a typical example of the life and circumstances of a child prodigy, and nice to imagine that many young children from poor families like his have managed to open up their lives in the way that Bidder was able to by drawing attention to his superior abilities. Sadly, however, that has only very rarely been the case. With respect to his family background, George Bidder was not at all typical of child prodigies. As it happens, the vast majority of cases of remarkable childhood precocity are found in educated and relatively wealthy homes.

A more typical child prodigy was Norbert Wiener, who eventually become one of the great mathematicians of the twentieth century. Wiener founded the science of cybernetics, which seeks to understand the principles underlying communication and control in both living and inorganic things. There is one point of similarity in the lives of Bidder and Wiener: in both cases their precocious achievements were partly mathematical. But in other respects the two men were very different. Norbert Wiener was born in 1894, to Jewish parents. His father, Leo Wiener, who had been born in Russia and had emigrated to the United States in 1880 at the age of eighteen (with only 50 cents in his pocket, he told his son), was fluent in a number of languages including German, French, Italian, Polish, Serbian, and modern Greek. Leo Wiener was a good classical scholar and an amateur mathematician as well: he wrote a number of articles on that subject. When Norbert was a young child the family moved to Boston, where his father eventually found a position at Harvard University.

Norbert Wiener's father was an enthusiastic man with a large number of interests, but he was also rather overbearing. And like James Mill, the father of John Stuart Mill, who was equally precocious in childhood, Leo Wiener was a hard taskmaster to his son. As a young child, Norbert was sent to a number of schools, but his parents found them all unsatisfactory. So when

Norbert was seven his father decided to take charge of his education. For the next several years most of the teaching was in the father's hands. Lessons with Leo Wiener were never exactly relaxed. His son remembered how,

> He would begin the discussion in an easy, conversational tone. This lasted exactly until I made the first mathematical mistake. Then the gentle and loving father was replaced by the avenger of the blood. (Wiener, 1953, p. 67)

When he came to read John Stuart Mill's description of his father's teaching, Norbert Wiener was well equipped to recognize the signs of a tyrannous parental regime, beneath the guarded 'proper Victorian' tone of Mill's account.

But if Norbert found his father to be a demanding and domineering teacher, he also saw much to like and admire in him. For all his faults, Leo Wiener was a warm and loving parent with many positive qualities. And

> my father was a romanticist… His righteousness partook of the element of *élan*, of triumph, of glorious and effective effort, of drinking deep of life… For me, a boy just starting life, this made him in many ways a noble and uplifting figure, a poet at heart… my taskmaster was at the same time my hero. (Wiener, 1953, p. 74)

From the beginning, Norbert's home life was filled with scholarly and intellectual events. His was a house of learning if ever there was one. He was given every encouragement to read. When he was very young his mother often read to him, and the child quickly realized that he could learn to read by himself. As soon as he could read he did read, from any book or magazine he could find to interest him.

Fortunately for Norbert, his parents had a large collection of books, and he was able to read anything he could discover on natural history, mathematics, and the physical sciences, as well as more obvious nourishments for a boy's imagination, such as *Treasure Island* and *The Arabian Nights*. Sometimes the father would bring his son books from the Harvard library. In this way Norbert acquired a book on the physics of light and electricity.

Helpfully, too, his father was friendly with some of the staff of the Boston Public Library. And the intellectualism of Norbert's home background was further augmented by the fact that many of the family's friends and neighbours were scholars.

With all the stimulation and encouragement he received from his father, and the many opportunities he had to see for himself how people went about scholarly activities and to learn to regard scholarship and studying as normal elements of everyday living, almost to be taken for granted as a routine part of home life, it is hardly surprising that Norbert Wiener gained the self-confidence to regard the pursuit of acquiring skills and knowledge as an activity that was always useful or necessary, often exciting, and certainly within his grasp.

When Norbert Wiener was 11 he began an undergraduate course at Tufts College (now Tufts University) in Medford, Massachusetts. He graduated with a bachelor's degree at the age of 14. He was still 14 when he became a graduate student at Harvard, where he gained his doctorate when he was 18. After a period abroad, during which he worked with Bertrand Russell, he returned to the United States. In 1919, he was appointed to a post at the Massachusetts Institute of Technology. He stayed there for 33 years, quickly establishing for himself a reputation as a leading mathematician.

This brief account may give the impression that Wiener's transition from the young *Wunderkind* into the eminent scientist was smooth and easy, even inevitable. In fact it was none of these. In his adolescence and early adulthood Wiener experienced troubles of many kinds, which left him frustrated, sometimes extremely depressed, and often in a mood of despair. For a start, he was a clumsy, short-sighted child. The early development of his abilities was highly uneven, with his social competence lagging several years behind his purely intellectual skills. He was not at all socially assured. Mixing with his classmates at school and college, most of whom were several years older than him, was never easy for the young Norbert Wiener.

As well as the social difficulties that any child prodigy might be expected to experience (see Radford, 1990), Norbert Wiener had many family problems. As we have seen, his father was a difficult man, demanding and overbearing. He expected a great deal from his son, but neither he nor his wife were prepared to give their son the freedom and independence that a talented youngster needed. Within the family, Norbert was for several years in the position of being an intellectual equal to his parents but treated like a child. He was financially, socially, and emotionally dependent on them, with no independent means of his own, and was given plenty of responsibilities but little authority. For example, he was expected to undertake much of the responsibility for educating his younger brother, Fritz, although he was never allowed to make any of the decisions about how the child would be taught, or permitted to discipline the spoiled and tiresome (in Norbert's view) younger sibling. Throughout his life he remained bitter about having been saddled with the job of teaching his brother.

Any young person needs to be given some independence and allowed to make his or her own mistakes, but Norbert's parents found it very difficult to let go of the reins. By his late adolescence it would clearly have been helpful for him to have been able to live on his own, away from the parental home of a family 'living too close together and driven in upon itself' (Wiener, 1953, p. 157). But the parents would hear none of this. His mother made it clear to him that his leaving home 'would be held against me for all eternity, as a sign of my ultimate failure, and would mean the complete and final collapse of family relations' (Wiener, 1953, p. 162). The youthful Norbert Wiener was never allowed to forget how much he depended on his family.

It is not at all easy to decide to what extent the problems with growing up that Norbert Wiener experienced were specifically caused by his being a child prodigy rather than simply by the difficulties that many adolescents have encountered, perhaps especially in close-knit Jewish immigrant families. Nor is it easy to be sure about causes and effects in George Bidder's early life. And if it is hard to answer such questions about individual child prodigies, it is even more difficult to discover general principles concerning important events in the lives of child prodigies in general. Nevertheless, we should make an effort to do so, particularly since it is becoming more and more common for parents nowadays to make enormous efforts to maximize their children's abilities.

The lives and achievements of child prodigies such as George Bidder and Norbert Wiener bring to our attention a number of issues concerning the origins of extraordinary human abilities and raise numerous questions.

With sufficient energy and dedication on the parents' part, it is possible that it may not be all that difficult to produce a child prodigy. What is considerably more difficult for parents to do is to bring up an individual who not only is precocious in childhood, but also grows up to be an adult who possesses personal qualities that enable him or her to make satisfyingly productive use of the special mental resources that an early start in life has made it possible to acquire. If parents have a good understanding of the circumstances that give rise to child prodigies, and are aware of the difficulties that precocious youngsters can encounter in the journey towards adulthood, they ought to be able to avoid at least some of the mistakes that have been made too often in the past by adults striving to maximize their offspring's mental powers.

Here are some of the questions child prodigies raise:

First, there are questions about the necessity for a person to be a prodigy in childhood if he or she is to become extraordinarily accomplished as a mature person. In order to be a genius, is it always necessary to start as a child prodigy? If not, is it necessary sometimes, and, if so, in what particular kinds of circumstances? In what ways may a person be helped in later life by having been a prodigy in childhood?

Second, in what ways do families contribute to a child's becoming extraordinarily precocious? Is it typically the case that one or more parent is strongly committed to providing an intensive early education, as happened in the childhood of Norbert Wiener? Do child prodigies sometimes emerge in families that are *not* unusually attentive to the child's early education?

Third, what kind of difficulties are child prodigies likely to experience? What unusual personal problems are likely to confront a person who has been a precocious child?

Fourth, what happens to child prodigies? Do most of them become remarkable adults, or do a large proportion 'burn out' or for one reason or another fail to maintain their early promise?

Fifth, at how early a stage in their lives do child prodigies begin to show their exceptionality? Does being seen to be extraordinary usually precede the special attention that is given to their early education, or is the reverse situation more typical, in which children become exceptional only after having already received special attention to their educational needs?

And sixth, how often do parental efforts to accelerate a child's progress actually succeed at all? Is it safe to assume that there are some children who, despite the most strenuous efforts of the parents to provide intense early education, never become at all exceptional? If this kind of failure does occur, in what circumstances is it more or less likely to happen?

These are just some of the questions that one would like to see answered, but supplying precise and definitive answers is no easy matter. There is no shortage of evidence: there are published accounts of a number of child prodigies, past and present, and some of these descriptions are highly informative and make fascinating reading. Essentially, there are three main reasons why it is so difficult to give firm answers to questions about the consequences and implications of a child being a prodigy. The first is that the sheer variety and variability of the many individuals to whom the word prodigy has been assigned restricts the extent to which it is possible to make general statements that apply to all or even the majority of them. The second reason is that the form of the evidence, most of which is to be found in biographical accounts of one kind or another, does not often make for precise quantitative statements. There are few of the facts or figures that would make it possible to make the kind of pronouncement which asserts that x per cent of child prodigies are this, or become that, or experience difficulties of such-and-such a kind.

The third source of difficulty is the fact that the label 'prodigy' has been applied somewhat imprecisely and inconsistently. Deciding who does and who does not belong in the prodigy category is not always possible. That is partly because the word has never been defined with sufficient precision, and partly because in real life the likelihood of someone being called a prodigy is affected by factors other than the degree to which their accomplishments are extraordinary. For example, it is much more likely that a child will be regarded as being a prodigy if he or she is exceptionally able in a way that is readily apparent to others than if the exceptionality is less obvious. So, for example, an outstanding young musician, or a tennis player, or a chess champion, whose special abilities come to the attention of a variety of adults, will have a greater likelihood than another child possessing abilities that are equally outstanding but of a more private and less readily displayed nature. Hence Mozart, whose remarkable early abilities were easily noticed, was widely regarded as being a child prodigy, while Einstein, whose abilities as a child were just as remarkable but not so obvious to other people, was not.

To be a genius, is it necessary to have been a child prodigy?

It is surprisingly hard to think of individuals who were considered to have been great thinkers as adults, but who gave no signs at all of exceptional precocity when they were children. Charles Darwin is one of the few geniuses who would definitely fall into this category. (So, perhaps, would Wordsworth and van Gogh.) But even Darwin, as a child, was never considered to be less than bright. And in his case it would be fair to point out that while he never drew attention to himself as being at all exceptional during his childhood, his early experiences and interests did provide a remarkably useful foundation for his later achievements. The fact that he was not considered to be outstanding as a child may have been due in part to his home background being an unusually intellectual one, and one in which the standards by which a child's abilities would have been rated were especially high. For the early development of an eminent biologist, the remarkably felicitous circumstances of Charles Darwin's life as a child and the strong continuities between his childhood interests and his adult preoccupations would have gone a long way to compensate for the absence of strikingly precocious early skills.

In all probability, among the substantial numbers of great scientists, scholars, artists, poets, dramatists, and novelists whose parents and teachers did not perceive in them any remarkable qualities when they were children, many did nevertheless possess abilities in childhood which were exceptional, albeit unrecognized. As I have already suggested, Albert

Einstein would appear to belong to this group. There is every indication that by the time he was 12 or 13 he had already acquired intellectual interests which reflected and drew upon resources of knowledge and understanding that would have been possessed by very few individuals of his age. At 12, he was reading serious books on the physical sciences and enjoyed talking about physics. He was also an enthusiastic and extremely precocious young mathematician.

Much has been made of Einstein's failure to be admitted to the Swiss Federal Polytechnic School in Zurich when he was 16. He was in fact two years younger than the normal age for entrance (Clark, 1979), which was the reason for his admission being delayed. Nevertheless, his assessors were very impressed by his performance. A better indication of his abilities as a 16-year-old is provided by a brilliant paper on electromagnetic phenomena which he produced at that age, 'Concerning the investigation of the state of aether in magnetic fields'. This displays the early beginnings of interests that were eventually to lead to massive achievements.

When is it an advantage to have been a prodigy? One circumstance in which being a child prodigy is especially likely to have practical utility for the individual is when poverty or other reasons would normally stand between a child and the educational opportunities that are necessary if the young person is to build on early achievements. By being sufficiently remarkable as a child, a young person may be drawn to the attention of those who have the money or the power to ensure that needed educational facilities or tuition are made available. This undoubtedly happened in the case of George Parker Bidder, for example. Nowadays, it is considerably more common than it was in Bidder's time, at least in wealthy countries, for children whose parents are poor to receive free or subsidized educational opportunities, but financial restrictions still prevent many young people from having access to advanced education.

In the Third World the situation is far worse. Even when a child is clearly recognized to be quite brilliant, there is no guarantee that the resources needed to make proper training possible will actually be provided. For example, in the case of the remarkable early twentieth-century Indian mathematician

Srinivasa Ramanujan, although he was acknowledged to be a child prodigy of immense ability, he was denied the support that would have made it possible for him to receive higher education. It was not until he was in his twenties, and working as an accounts clerk, that the Cambridge mathematician G. H. Hardy (to whom Ramanujan had sent a portfolio of his work) was able to put into motion the wheels that led to Ramanujan being able to pursue his work on a full-time basis in a university environment. Had the young Ramanujan been given the kind of education that he deserved, his contribution to mathematics would in all probability have been considerably greater than it was. Doubtless there are many thousands of young prodigies who are similarly deprived of opportunities to gain remarkable abilities that could benefit mankind.

If money is short, drawing attention to oneself as a child prodigy can be an effective way of starting a career, even if it does not directly open the way to opportunities for advanced education. As we have seen, one of the immediate consequences of George Bidder's performances was to augment the family's income. In Mozart's time, when good musicians were two-a-penny, it was not at all easy to climb above the ranks of the numerous other ill-paid performers. As his father had calculated, the young Mozart's spectacular exhibitions as a child gave him a valuable early advantage over the competition.

In certain fields of human endeavour the training and preparation that are essential for reaching the highest levels of achievement demand resources that are particularly scarce or hard to obtain, or sufficiently expensive to be beyond the means of even those parents whose financial position is relatively sound. For example, to become a top-ranking concert pianist it is essential for the young performer to receive tuition from one of a very small number of distinguished master teachers. But these individuals are prepared to offer their services only to pupils whom they consider to be unusually promising. So, finding such a teacher is a hurdle that a young performer can only surmount if he or she is already extremely accomplished when still quite young. Similarly, in order to become a world-class tennis player it is important to be able to practise all year, and a young player can expect to meet fierce competition for the limited funds that are available to help make this possible. Therefore, only those individuals who have come a long way towards excellence while they are still young will be in a strong position to compete for the funds that are needed in order to gain access to the training facilities on which future progress depends.

There is a sense in which the children of rich parents can better afford not to be child prodigies. Individuals who are particularly wealthy are to some extent immune from the necessity to draw attention to themselves and make career choices while they are still very young. Tolstoy, for instance, a rich man who was always able to find money to pay his gambling debts, could afford to spend his early years sampling a variety of occupations before settling down in his forties to write novels. William James was able to depend on his father's wealth while he vacillated for several years before deciding to devote his life to the study of philosophy and psychology.

Finally, there are a few fields of scholarship where, in addition to the necessity of maintaining a single-minded commitment over a period of many years in order to reach the highest levels of excellence, circumstances are such that it is unlikely that such a commitment will endure into the middle years of life. From then on, even the most wholeheartedly dedicated of individuals increasingly begin to look outside any particular narrow pursuit, and to take an interest in family matters and wider concerns. Consequently, many of those achievements that depend upon the individual narrowly and single-mindedly concentrating on a particular problem over a period of years are likely to be made fairly early in life. Mathematicians, for example, tend to produce their best and most important work in their twenties and thirties (Roe, 1952; Lehman, 1953). In order to be in a position to reach one's peak by this time, it is necessary for an individual already to have reached a high level of expertise by around the late teens. So only if a person has made an early start towards becoming a distinguished mathematician will he or she stand a reasonable chance of being highly successful. As it happens, it is rare nowadays to find very young children who are recognized as being prodigies in the field of mathematics: it is more usual for young mathematicians to begin to show exceptional competence when they are well into their second decade.

How do families contribute to childhood precocity?

In Chapter 2 we discovered that the home backgrounds of the majority of extraordinarily able individuals have been fairly cultured and intellectually stimulating ones. It would be very surprising if that was not equally true of the backgrounds of those extraordinary people who began to exhibit remarkable abilities while they were still children. Indeed, it is true: most child prodigies emerge in circumstances where the parents are educated, concerned about their children's early education, and both willing and able to make a larger-than-average practical contribution towards providing their children with opportunities to learn.

In a survey of research into the contribution of childhood experience to the development of precocity, William Fowler (1981) described an early study by Root, who found that 87 per cent of a sample of gifted children aged between six and 13, whose IQ scores averaged 160, had been given an exceptionally large amount of training at home, by the parents. Typically, the mother had devoted a large proportion of her time to preschool education. Some of the mothers in the study are described as exhibiting 'unbounded ambitions and hopes and persistence' concerning their aspirations for their sons and daughters. Eighty per cent of the fathers were in professional or semi-professional occupations. Root's interviews established that virtually all the parents had high expectations for their children. The latter were expected to achieve high standards at intellectual tasks. They were given every encouragement to be successful, at home and at school. The parents displayed considerable pride in their children and made ambitious plans for them. They placed stress on helping their sons and daughters to gain language skills. These parents seem to have had an intuitive understanding of the fact that parents who augment a young child's experiences with language may thereby make an enormous contribution to intellectual development. Such parents were unusually willing to treat the children as intelligent and rational people, rather than talking down to them as some parents do. All the parents seemed to have placed considerable emphasis on the importance of reading, and most of their children had learned to read by the age of three.

By and large, these findings have been repeated in every subsequent investigation of the family circumstances of intellectually precocious children. More recent investigations, such as the Chicago-based studies of exceptional young people who were making careers in a number of scientific, artistic, and sporting professions, as well as David Feldman's intensive examination of the day-to-day lives of six remarkable child prodigies (Feldman, 1986) and Sloboda and Howe's (1991) research into the backgrounds of young muscians, agree with the earlier reports in finding that most parents of child prodigies are unusually anxious for their children to do well, and able and willing to invest a substantial amount of effort into helping their children to make early progress.

It is interesting to find that essentially similar results were obtained from the large-scale study that Lewis Terman initiated in California at the beginning of the twentieth century in order to examine highly intelligent children's backgrounds, despite the fact that Terman believed environmental influences to be comparatively unimportant. With considerable uniformity, the results of case after case yield clear documentation of the parents having provided unusually intensive intellectual stimulation in early childhood. Even in those few instances where parental responses to interviews or questionnaires provide no direct evidence that exceptional amounts of early childhood training were given, there are usually clues that permit one to infer that the parents nevertheless devoted considerable amounts of time and attention to the child's early education.

Parents sometimes deny that their unusually able child received any special attention, but such denials cannot always be taken at face value, Fowler (1981) quotes from a mother's account of a child prodigy, who, according to her, developed remarkable abilities quite spontaneously, with virtually no help at all from the parent. This mother claimed to have resisted any temptation to provide teaching, or even encouragement or assistance, to her child, whose accomplishments were, according to the mother, entirely self-initiated. Fowler points out that, in spite of all these firm denials, the detailed record clearly reveals that this child actually received a great deal of training and stimulation. Belying the impression that the mother acted in a purely passive capacity, content simply to sit back and wonder at the miracle of her child's spontaneously developing powers, Fowler notes that both parents were in fact sufficiently involved in the child's early education to keep an astonishingly detailed record of her achievements. As he tartly notes, these parents actually kept an exact record of the child's vocabulary (229 words at 16 months) and at age five, listing and classifying into parts of speech every single one of her 6 837 words over a six-month period (Fowler, 1981, p. 355). Another situation in which the parents in all probability gave their child intensive early stimulation, while vehemently denying that they did so, is revealed in a claim by the parents that they first learned of their daughter's ability to read when they discovered her reading *Heidi* at the age of four. The truth of this claim is thrown into the question by the fact that these parents, too, kept meticulous records of their daughter's accomplishments, such as the exact letters she had learned at particular ages, the age at which she first mastered the alphabet, acquired counting skills, recognized colours, and so on.

There are a number of possible reasons for certain parents having been so reluctant to admit to having taken a major role in training their children. Some parents have wanted to believe that their child's unusual development reflected the spontaneous unfolding of inherited native endowments. For a few parents, a contributing factor may have been the wish to portray their child's powers as being not simply exceptional but unique, and perhaps miraculous as well, conceivably a sign that the child has been specially 'chosen' by a supernatural deity. Whatever the reasons for parents' reluctance to admit their own role, it is important to be aware that such reluctance is sometimes encountered, and to acknowledge that in child prodigies the absence of a record of intensive early stimulation cannot be taken as firm evidence that no special training actually took place.

Does the degree of formality of parental training matter? Parents who are similar to one another in the amounts of time they invest in helping and encouraging their children are likely to differ considerably in the actual teaching procedures they adopt. One dimension – to be more accurate, a constellation of related dimensions – along which equally committed parents may differ concerns the degree to which instruction is structured or formally planned. Certain parents of child prodigies, for instance James Mill and (to a lesser extent) Leo Wiener, have clearly planned their children's early education in some detail. They have deliberately provided a regimen of carefully sequenced training and instruction, and have required the child to practise at tasks allotted by the parent. Other parents have been much less systematic, either by accident or design, more inclined to take their cues from the child's own curiosity, and generally more 'child-centred'.

Does the degree of formality of parental teaching activities make a difference, so far as the child's learning is concerned? Are there grounds for stating that the efforts of parents whose approach to early childhood education is a relatively formal and pre-planned one are either more or less successful than the efforts of parents who do not plan their child's early education so formally or systematically? Are there any research findings that justify advising parents to adopt a particular kind of teaching strategy?

It seems not. William Fowler (1981) carefully sifted the evidence from many investigations in an effort to answer this question, but he encountered a number of difficulties. One problem is that the teaching methods that parents actually use are not uniformly formal or informal across different situations. And even when it is possible for researchers to observe the teaching that is given, the approach cannot always be classified as straightforwardly formal or informal. Another problem is that the different approaches adopted by parents do not simply indicate the choice of alternative procedures for reaching identical goals: the varying approaches may also reflect differences in parental attitudes and philosophies, or in their beliefs about the causes of exceptional human abilities. So it would be naïve to assume that in looking at the progress of children whose parents have taken different approaches to early childhood education one is observing the effects of a natural experiment that provides a straightforward comparison between like and like, one in which the instructional method is the only parameter that varies.

Still, we can look to see whether or not there do exist any dissimilarities in young people's progress that are reliably associated with disparities in parental approaches, even if the above-mentioned complications dictate that we would not be justified in inferring that any observed contrasts in children's cognitive growth would supply proof of the differing effectiveness of alternative methods. But as it happens, there appear to be no differences in children's abilities that are systematically related in any way at all to dissimilarities in the particular teaching methods adopted by parents who are equally committed to the early education of their children.

Is it possible to become a child prodigy without parental involvement? The fact that there is evidence of an unusual degree of parental involvement in the early training of the vast majority of child prodigies and other children whose intelligence test scores indicate precocious early intellectual development, prompts the following questions: Is it possible to be a child prodigy in the absence of considerable involvement on the part of parents or other adults? Are there any child prodigies whose education in early childhood has not been unusually intense?

It is certainly difficult, if not impossible, to locate such cases, especially if one is careful to avoid being misled by unreliable parental disclaimers. None of the many case histories reported in Fowler's survey provides convincing evidence of extraordinary precocity in the absence of adult involvement. Nor do any of the reports concerning the many subjects interviewed by the Chicago team. Nor do any of David Feldman's reports. In searching for exceptions, two possible directions seem especially promising. First, there have been a few eminent individuals who, according to biographical evidence that is readily available, experienced remarkably bleak and unstimulating childhoods. The case of the writer H. G. Wells, who is nowadays best known for his prophetic novels such as *The Time Machine*, but also made important contributions as a social thinker and an influential popularizer of scientific knowledge, seems to fit into this category. The second promising direction in which to look for possible cases of child prodigies who have received no intensive education in early childhood is among the ranks of mathematical child prodigies. In at least some respects, the young mathematician can be considerably more self-sufficient than a child whose talents lie in other fields. Compared with, say, either a would-be young reader, or a musical child prodigy, whose early progress depends to a very considerable extent on the teaching that is available, a child who has become interested in numbers can forge ahead with a considerable degree of independence and autonomy.

H. G. Wells's childhood was particularly interesting. He was a remarkably precocious child despite the fact that he was brought up in conditions of considerable penury. His parents were unhappy, unsuccessful, and not well educated. Their relationship was somewhat rancorous and bitter. His mother had been a lady's maid until she married his father, an under-gardener who worked on a country estate. During Wells's early childhood they struggled, with very little success, to make more than a bare living (MacKenzie and MacKenzie, 1973). Their house, much of which was below ground level, was squeezed between a haberdasher's shop and a tailor's workshop.

But a closer look at the actual details of H. G. Wells's childhood reveals a portrait that is subtly different from the picture that we see at first glance, and not nearly so bleak. And the differences are ones that would have been crucial for a child's early intellectual development. Examining his childhood slightly more closely serves to illuminate how very greatly our understanding of someone's early progress can be changed by switching from a relatively superficial observation of the individual's first years to a deeper examination. This insight provides a useful reminder of the need to be wary about taking at face value the kinds of biographical information about people's childhood years that are most readily available and most easily quantified. Investigations that neglect to make proper use of those pieces of evidence about individuals that are too subtle, either to be readily quantified or to be detected by relatively coarse-netted techniques of observation and measurement, may produce highly distorted accounts of the true state of affairs.

In Wells's case, a closer look at his family life reveals that his father, although a bit of a dreamer, never very successful at the jobs he took on, and too restless to be other than dissatisfied with his lot, was nevertheless a thoughtful and intelligent man who had made considerable efforts to extend his knowledge. Throughout his life he was a keen reader. (He had his moments of glory. He sometimes played cricket for Kent and, on 26 June,

1862, he clean bowled four Sussex batsmen in four successive balls. Joseph Wells had an attractive personality and considerable charm. His feats at cricket made him something of a local celebrity and brought him regular employment in a coaching job at a nearby school.

Also, despite the penuriousness of the family background, by the standards of its time it was not entirely lacking in intellectual stimulation for a young child. For a woman of her social background, Wells's mother was most unusual in that she kept a daily diary. She taught her son to count when he was quite small. She also hung up large letters from the alphabet in the kitchen, and the child was sent to school from the age of five. And when, at seven, he was laid up for some weeks with a broken leg, he discovered the joy of reading, and his parents kept him supplied with all the books he could have wished for.

Details like these give us a fresh and very different perspective on Wells's early life. We can see that Wells's background was not, after all, quite such a barren environment for a child's first years. Also, Wells was lucky with his schools. A number of the teachers he encountered were astute enough to spot his early promise.

Another promising area to search for cases of child prodigies who are exceptions to the general finding that extraordinary childhood precocity is only found when there is marked adult involvement in the child's mental development, is among the ranks of mathematicians. Although rare nowadays, mathematical child prodigies were less unusual in the past, largely because it has always been possible for children to acquire impressive mental calculating skills, if they are willing to practise enough. In previous centuries a considerable number of mathematicians have been highly skilled at doing mental calculations, and have acquired that ability when they were children. Gauss and Leibnitz are examples of such individuals. In the present century, the incentives for a child acquiring skills of that kind have lessened. This is partly because – especially since the advent of electronic calculators – the practical value of possessing calculating skills has diminished. Also, as the nature of mathematics has changed over the years, the importance of mental calculating abilities as a stepping-stone to more advanced aspects of mathematics has diminished. (A modern equivalent to a nineteenth-century calculating prodigy might be the kind of youngster who creates intricate computer games.)

The individual who is making progress at learning to be a mathematician can be more independent and self-sufficient than is possible for learners who are working in other fields of knowledge (Stanley *et al.*, 1977; Marjoram and Nelson, 1985). Jacques Inaudi sharpened his mathematical abilities as he worked as an illiterate shepherd boy (Smith, 1983), and Ramanujan rediscovered on his own large segments of the mathematical knowledge that has been acquired in recent centuries. Even so, the home backgrounds of the vast majority of great mathematicians have been ones in which either there exists direct evidence that special early stimulation was provided or there are strong reasons for our inferring that. For instance, evidence collected by William Fowler (1986) shows that among a sample of 25 'historically recognized great math-ematicians' there was firm evidence of 21 of them having been given special early stimulation. Facts about the early lives of the other four are sparse, but it is known that three of them were brought up in cultured families. Contradictory accounts have appeared of the childhood of Carl Friedrich Gauss, one of the greatest mathematicians of all time. The contradictions draw attention to one of the problems encountered with biog-raphical evidence. It is has been claimed by one recent author, Amy Wallace, that Gauss's father was 'a poor, uncouth laborer' and was reluctant to allow his son to be educated (Wallace, 1986). But in an article published in the same year in which Wallace's book appeared, another author describes Gauss's father as having been an accountant. and a fine calculator and a good writer (Fowler, 1986). As a child, Gauss was a brilliant prodigy and his mental calculating was quite remarkable. Despite the father's apparent lack of enthusiasm, the circum-stances of Gauss's early home life may not have been at all unstimulating or unsupportive. It is known that Gauss had an uncle who probably made a large contribution to the child's early education, and did a great deal to encourage him. Gauss's mother took great pride in her son. In summary, it seems likely that in most if not all of the cases where first appearances suggest that a child prodigy has emerged in the absence of any stimulation or encouragement at all, a closer examination of the child's circumstances would reveal – as in Wells's case – that one or more individuals have in fact given the child a substantial amount of help.

What special difficulties and problems do child prodigies experience?

By definition, child prodigies are unusual children. If only because of this, it would be surprising if they experienced no unusual difficulties at all. But it would be wrong to deduce that growing up must always be more difficult for a child prodigy than for an 'ordinary' child. In fact, the evidence indicates that children who gain unusually high scores on intelligence tests, such as the participants in Terman's large-scale Californian study, are on the whole less, rather than more, likely than others to experience severe personal problems in childhood and adolescence.

Nevertheless, there are certain kinds of childhood difficulties to which child prodigies are particularly prone. First, many child prodigies have had to cope with unusual parental pressures of one kind or another. That is not to say that all parents of child prodigies have placed unreasonable demands on their children, nor to deny that many children who have not been prodigies have had very demanding parents. All the same, it is true that the parents, especially the fathers, of child prodigies have often been people who have not only expected a great deal of their children, but have made that quite obvious to the children concerned.

Norbert Wiener was one child prodigy who saw his father as a demanding taskmaster. In his different way, James Mill made his son's childhood difficult and stressful. Mozart and his talented older sister, Nannerl, were almost certainly subjected to a good deal of pressure from their father, who was excessively anxious to display their exceptionality to the world. It is possible that contemporary child prodigies are less likely to experience unreasonable parental demands to excel than prodigies in previous generations, if only because there is widespread agreement nowadays about the undesirability of 'pressurizing' young children. Certainly, in none of the detailed case histories provided by David Feldman (1986) is there evidence of excessive parental pressure, and the same is generally true of the much larger sample of highly successful young adults examined in the Chicago studies. (Some of those individuals, but not all, could be said to have been prodigies when they were children.) Although it is clear that many of the parents studied by the Chicago-based authors were very keen for their children to do well and encouraged them to set high standards for themselves, the investigations unearthed few obvious signs of parents making unreasonable demands.

On the other hand, some descriptions of contemporary ex-prodigies do point to the likelihood of there having been sufficient parental pressure during childhood to have had adverse effects on the individual. As we saw earlier, Norbert Wiener's autobiography makes it clear that as well as the 'pressure to succeed' imposed by some anxious parents, families may inflict other kinds of pressures that can be oppressive, and make it very difficult for the young person to enjoy an independent and self-directed life. The words that describe the less attractive aspects of the Wiener family – close, claustrophobic, demanding, intense, judgemental, inward-looking – hint at some of the negative qualities that are not uncommon in parents of child prodigies. These parents invariably identify somewhat closely with their children and take the keenest interest in their progress. Difficulties arise when the degree of identification is such that parents start to live their own lives through the child. This is especially likely to happen if the parents' own early hopes have been frustrated. For a parent who is trying too hard to shape a child's destiny, the growing child's natural desire to become more independent and free from parental control may be seen as a kind of rejection, which threatens to destroy the desired state of affairs in which the parent's own needs are being met by the child's activities. The kinds of family circumstances in which children appear to be over-dependent on their parents are often ones in which strong dependencies operate in more than one direction: parents and children are each unhealthily dependent on the other. The parents' unwillingness to let their sons and daughters live their own lives is a sign of the parents' own abnormal dependence on the children.

Another cause of difficulties for child prodigies is that, especially among children, an individual who is very unusual may be seen as freakish and alien. Exceptionally able children are likely to be different from others in a number of ways, if only because their values and interests are not those of an ordinary child (Fox, 1976; Keating, 1976; Freeman, 1985).

Most children like to have friends of their own age. They want to feel that they are accepted by their peers. It is a harsh fact of life that ordinary children tend to be intolerant of other children whom they perceive as being odd or peculiar. Of course, some child prodigies get on very well with their schoolmates. Prodigies who have well-developed social skills, and are unusual only in being exceptionally able, do not find that precocity on its own produces crushing difficulties for them.

Typically, however, the very circumstances that make a child exceptionally precocious lead to the child being unusual in other respects. The parents' values and interests may contrast with those of the families of a prodigy's peers and have the effect of restricting the extent to which the child can enjoy interests that are shared with others, shared knowledge of the world outside school, shared attitudes, and shared values. All of these serve to oil the wheels of social intercourse and make it easy to form friendships. Consequently, a child who rarely watches television will lack one useful point of contact for casual social encounters and easy interactions with classmates. On its own, the effects of being different in a small way like this are relatively trivial and form no major obstacle, but the combined effect of being unlike one's peers in a number of ways, even small ones, may be to make it quite hard for a young prodigy to form comfortable social relationships with other children.

At school, the fact that an intellectually precocious child may be placed in a class in which most of the pupils are considerably older can lead to further difficulties. It is never easy for a young person to be fully accepted by others who are more socially mature. Life at school may be especially hard for an individual who is smaller than most classmates and relatively incompetent at some valued activities, such as sports and games.

Not every child prodigy will experience the problems I have mentioned, but biographical accounts show that these kinds of difficulty are not at all uncommon. For instance, a number of the many problems that Norbert Wiener experienced during childhood and adolescence stemmed from the fact that others regarded him as being different from themselves, and he was not helped by being a short-sighted and clumsy child. His contemporary, William Sidis, an acquaintance of Wiener who attended Harvard at the same time but was never able to make the transition from being a brilliant child prodigy to becoming an adult capable of making productive use of his talents, was similarly harassed by problems that were rooted in the fact that he was so very different from other young people of a similar age.

Other problems can arise because people often underestimate the extent to which it is possible for an individual to possess particular skills in isolation from other abilities. It is quite possible, for instance, for someone to be a brilliant chess player, or a superb musician, or an excellent mathematician, while having less than average ability at other intellectual skills, including ones that might appear closely related to the field in which he or she excels.

The abilities of child prodigies are often highly specialized. Prodigies' intellectual development, compared with that of most ordinary people, can be highly uneven in ways that confound the expectations that people may have formed on the basis of a child's superior abilities in one area. It can be rather disconcerting to find that a ten-year-old whose mathematical expertise is on a par with that of an exceptionally able adult may have the social maturity of an eight-year-old or the sense of humour of a six-year-old. Quite a number of child prodigies have run into troubles that have been caused by their failure to live up to people's unrealistic expectations that their special abilities would be matched by comparable superiority in quite different areas of competence.

The fact that child prodigies do tend to specialize can also produce consequences that follow directly from the fact that specializing at one activity inevitably limits the time available for other potentially valuable activities. A child who is practising at the piano for eight hours a day cannot simultaneously be learning biology or mathematics. In addition, leisure hours may be sharply curtailed, and that can create problems, because children do learn from watching television, reading novels, taking an interest in sports, enjoying leisurely conversations with their friends and engaging in social activities of one kind or another, and other kinds of relaxed spare-time occupations. Reading novels can help a child to gain wisdom, humility, a sense of humour, awareness of the needs and feelings of other people, and many varieties of insights into the human condition. So it would be wrong to assume that an individual whose time-filling specialized interests seriously curtail these alternative kinds of activities will be at no disadvantage at all (Howe, 1977).

For some child prodigies, the attention of media journalists and the resulting publicity can create real difficulties. Some contemporary and recent prodigies have been clearly upset by the attention they have received, and previous generations have also suffered. Adding to Norbert Wiener's problems with the press was the fact that his own father seemed to welcome all this attention. Leo Wiener liked to sound off at length, either in interviews or articles, in which he expounded his educational theories and was at pains to emphasize, to his son's embarrassment, that Norbert was just a quite ordinary boy whose successes were entirely due to the superlative education his father was giving him. But the troubles Norbert Wiener experienced in connection with the attention of the press were trivial compared with those which assaulted his acquaintance and contemporary, William Sidis. Sidis was often hounded by reporters, and ridiculed in cruelly hostile newspaper articles. In Sidis's case it would be fair to say that the unhappiness caused to him by the unwelcome attentions of the press was one reason for Sidis, who was just as brilliant an adolescent as Norbert Wiener, failing to follow up his early promise with a productive and successful adult career. Frequent newspaper reports on him appeared throughout his childhood. The tone of these articles was generally friendly at first, but as time went on the press coverage of William Sidis became increasingly hostile. Sadly, Sidis continued to be a target for hostile journalism even when his days of early promise were long past and he was living a quiet life of simple poverty and wanted only to be left alone.

What happens to child prodigies when they become adults?

The majority of child prodigies do become unusually capable adults who enjoy productive and successful lives. Of course, the prodigies whose feats are most spectacular do not necessarily eventually achieve the highest levels of eminence. To take the case of two brothers, for instance, the sons of James Thomson (a teacher of mathematics and a writer of textbooks who became a professor at Glasgow University) were both child prodigies. But while the older brother, James, had the most glittering childhood, won several prizes at the University when he was still in his early teens, and died with the reputation of being a highly distinguished engineer, his minor fame was eclipsed by that of his younger brother, William. The latter's less dazzling childhood was followed by a brilliant scientific career, as a result of which he became Lord Kelvin, and was one of the greatest of nineteenth-century physicists.

Although a substantial number of child prodigies have gone on to highly distinguished adult careers, and a few have dramatically failed to live up to their early promise, the vast majority of ex-prodigies are moderately successful and happy enough, but are neither outstandingly successful nor sufficiently extraordinary in other ways to draw much attention to themselves. This state of affairs may be inevitable, if only because the numbers of children who are described as being prodigies are simply larger, as a proportion of the population as a whole, than the numbers of adults who become famed or well known by virtue of their outstanding intellectual qualities. After all, there are only so many Nobel prizes and Olympic gold medals to go around, and the public's appetite for names on whom to bestow the reputation of being famous is not unlimited. So it comes as no surprise to find that investigations which have examined the subsequent lives of large samples of intellectually precocious or 'gifted' children, such as the Californian individuals whose lives were followed in the large-scale research study initiated by Lewis Terman, have found that the majority of gifted children enjoy careers that are reasonably successful but not earth-shattering. None of the 1500 children who participated in that study became a Nobel prize winner. But there were some prominent scientists among them, and several judges, a distinguished film director, at least one well-known writer, and substantial numbers of scholars, doctors, and lawyers.

Why are some ex-prodigies, in adulthood, more successful than others? It is not always easy to say just why things turn out better for some individuals than for others. Although a child's cleverness or the brilliance of his or her intellectual powers may be enough to ensure that the child is labelled as a prodigy, the success of an adult career never depends on these qualities alone. Among the other determinants of later success are factors such as temperament, personality, self-confidence, strength of commitment to a goal, social skills, and the ability to communicate with other people. And luck can also play a part. So the attributes that may suffice to ensure that a child is regarded as a prodigy are not, on their own, sufficient to guarantee that the same individual will prove to be an unusually capable adult. Also, some of the crucial factors have less to do with the individual's abilities as such, than with events in the outside world that determine how the person's accomplishments will be received by other people.

The difficulty of explaining just why one prodigy becomes an eminent adult and another does not is illustrated by comparing two individuals who in some respects were remarkably similar to each other. Two years before the birth of George Bidder, a child named Zerah Colburn was born in the American state of Vermont. Like Bidder, Colburn was a remarkable juvenile calculating prodigy (Smith, 1983). Like Bidder (whom Colburn met on one occasion, when Colburn was probably 14 and Bidder 12, Colburn first drew the attention of adults to his talent when he was about six years of age. At that time his father heard him repeating multiplication tables to himself, although the child had only attended the local school for a few weeks. When the father asked his son to multiply 13 x 97 he was immediately given the correct answer, 1261. Like Bidder, the young Colburn travelled round the country giving public demonstrations of his abilities.

And like Bidder, Colburn came to the attention of wealthy individuals who were willing to pay for his education. He was offered a number of opportunities that would have made it possible for him to make himself into a highly educated young person. His early precocity was even more marked than Bidder's. When he was still only six he could solve problems requiring him to state the number of seconds in 2000 years, to give the product of 12 225 multiplied by 1223, and the square of 1449. A year later it took him precisely six seconds to state the number of hours in 38 years, two months and seven days. At the age of only nine he became one of the first mathematicians to establish whether or not certain very large numbers were primes, and his ability to factorize considerably surpassed Bidder's.

Yet, unlike George Bidder, the adult Zerah Colburn never came to much in the world's eyes. It is not easy see why, with such similar abilities, the two men should have enjoyed such contrasting degrees of success. By all accounts Colburn was an outgoing man, and personable enough. He was clearly intelligent. At different times in his short life he was a mathematician employed to make astronomical calculations, a teacher of literature and modern and classical languages, an actor, and a minister of religion. Yet most of his adult life was unhappy, and he lived in poverty. When he died at the age of only 35 there was none of the acclaim and praise that followed Bidder's death.

Granted that riches and material success are not the only measures of a life's worth, and that Colburn could hardly have accomplished in 35 years achievements equal to those of Bidder's 72-year life span, it still remains a puzzle why the two men, of seemingly equal talents, should have had such different fortunes. Perhaps it was largely a matter of chance favouring the one and not the other. Bidder's remarkable energy and vitality may have made a difference, or perhaps his greater worldliness was a significant factor in his greater success, compared with Colburn's. Despite being a bold and outspoken individual, Bidder appears to have had a good eye for the main chance and a willingness to conform when doing so was in his interest. Bidder's temperament and his abilities seem to have been well matched. Compared with him, Colburn seems to have been something of a lonely wanderer, perhaps rather a lost soul after his father's death in 1824, and with little of the dynamism and panache that Bidder employed in the management of his own career.

One factor that makes it difficult to explain why some ex-prodigies have much more success in their adult lives than others is that making comparisons between individuals generally involves comparing people who have been born in different places, at different times, and whose cultural backgrounds have been different in a number of respects. When there are a large number of dimensions on which people differ from one another, it may be impossible to discover which of those dimensions are most crucial. For this reason it would be helpful to have an opportunity to compare a number of prodigies who have been brought up in circumstances which, in some respects at least, are not dissimilar.

Fortunately, some relevant information became available as a result of a situation that came about in the Boston area, early in the present century. In the year 1909, no less than five child prodigies were enrolled at Harvard. Norbert Wiener was one. William Sidis was another. The third was Adolf Berle, a more outgoing and socially accomplished child than either Wiener or Sidis. Berle, whose brother and two sisters were also exceptionally able (one sister, Lina, learned to speak several languages by the age of three), had a dazzling career as a lawyer, becoming Assistant Secretary of State under Franklin D. Roosevelt (Wallace, 1986). The fourth child prodigy was Roger Sessions, who became a well-known composer, and lived until 1985. Cedric Wing Houghton, the fifth, died before graduating.

Except for Sidis, the four who lived into adulthood all had highly productive lives. William Sidis, as we have seen, was never able to make use of his remarkable abilities. According to Norbert Wiener, Sidis developed a resentment against science, mathematics, and all that his family stood for, as well as 'a hatred for anything that might put him in a position of responsibility and give him the need to make decisions' (Wiener, 1953, p. 132).

It is not difficult to find reasons for Sidis's failure to enjoy a happy and productive adulthood. His childhood would have been difficult enough even without the press attention that, as I have already said, helped to destroy his self-confidence. His dependence on his parents was even greater than Wiener's. As we saw earlier, Wiener only just managed to detach himself sufficiently from his parents' control to create a life for himself:

some brilliant young prodigies have failed to make the necessary break. For example, even when he was 18, Erwin Nyiregyhazi, the dazzling Hungarian pianist, could not feed or dress himself properly, or tie his own shoes (Feldman, 1986). Sidis was equally unable to look after himself properly. With his appalling lack of social skills and his inability to keep himself clean or dress himself, he was ill-equipped for a fully independent life. Yet he resented his dependence on his parents, and the resentment grew to hatred. He refused to attend his father's funeral. Towards his mother, a domineering and by all accounts appalling woman in some ways, he developed an intense loathing.

The comparison between Wiener and Sidis is especially interesting because their backgrounds were remarkably similar. The parents of both of them were ambitious and successful recent Jewish immigrants to the United States. Both fathers were Russian, were themselves intellectually precocious, and both arrived in America in the 1880s. Both men were fiery, energetic, dominating, and somewhat overbearing. In photographs they even look alike. Both had strong (and similar) ideas about the education of children. Strangely, however, while Leo Wiener put almost as much energy into the education of his daughter, Sarah – who developed into an extremely capable person – and the youngest child, Fritz, as he did into his elder son's, Boris Sidis paid remarkably little attention to the early education of his daughter, Helena.

Boris Sidis was no ogre. He was not knowingly cruel to his son and his teaching methods seem to have been less harsh than those of either James Mill or Leo Wiener. And the education he gave his son was neither narrow nor unenlightened. In theory at least, he strongly opposed the use of any compulsion or pressure, and was in favour of taking cues from the child's own curiosity.

Intellectually, the training that William Sidis gained from his parents was magnificent, but for a number of reasons he never achieved what had been expected of him. One reason was that his parents were too concerned with their educational theories to pay sufficient attention to the emotional, non-intellectual needs of their growing son. Although they gave him plenty of their time and showed him off at every opportunity, they failed to see just how uneven his development was. They also neglected to make sure that he was properly equipped with the personal and social skills that are necessary for survival in the harsh world outside the protected environment of home. And whereas Norbert Wiener learned in childhood to enjoy a number of healthy outdoor interests, and went on long nature walks and hiking expeditions with his father, Boris Sidis was so opposed to all non-intellectual pursuits (he talked of 'meaningless games and silly, objectless sports') that the young William never had a chance to acquire the kinds of habits and interests that most well-rounded people depend upon for relaxing the mind and fortifying the body. Most importantly, his parents completely failed to equip him to deal with all the public attention that came his way.

Even more damaging to William Sidis's sense of ease and self-confidence was the fact that his parents' marriage, unlike that of the Wieners, was not at all happy. For this there were a number of causes. Neither Boris Sidis nor his wife can have been easy to live with, although it was the mother, who appears to have been bad-tempered, humourless, and domineering, always nagging and criticizing her son, whom William grew to dislike the most strongly, and who did most to undermine his fragile confidence in himself.

The adult William Sidis failed to make real use of his abilities because, although there was little wrong with his intellect, his childhood left him frightened and unhappy, neither self-confident enough nor sufficiently at peace with himself to rely on his intellectual powers. They stayed largely unused until his death in 1944 at the age of 46. With hindsight, is easy to say that Sidis might have made an enormous contribution if only his parents had done more to make him self-sufficient and independent, instead of concentrating on his intellect to the neglect of matters that are equally important. Any parents of a prodigy might do well to keep in mind the words of an earlier prodigy's father, the elder Karl Witte, who wrote,

But let me tell what I wanted to make of him; then it will appear of itself what I did not want him to become. I wanted to educate him to be a man in the noblest sense of the word. So far as I in my circumstances could do so and was aided in this matter by my knowledge and experience, he was first of all to be a healthy, strong, active, and happy young man, and in this, as everybody knows, I have succeeded. He was to enter manhood with this invaluable equipment. He was to develop his bodily powers to the utmost extent and yet harmoniously, even as he should do with his intellectual powers. (Witte, 1975, pp. 63–4)

Norbert Wiener only just learned to stand on his own feet. William Sidis never did. Some of the greatest of ex-prodigies – Wiener himself, for example, and John Ruskin and John Stuart Mill as well – bore throughout their lives the scars of having been too dependent on over-demanding parents. The parents of today's prodigies would do well to take note of Witte's good sense.

At how early a stage do prodigies begin to display their exceptionality?

According to the accounts that are available, most of those individuals who have been recognized as being prodigies in childhood and have also been exceptionally accomplished people when they became adults did not display any unusual precocity in their earliest months. On the contrary, with remarkable uniformity, the parents of a number of the most impressive child prodigies of all, including Karl Witte, John Stuart Mill, Norbert Wiener, and William Sidis, have insisted on the sheer ordinariness of their infants. James Mill, for example, regarded his son's ability to learn as no better than average. As the latter recorded in his *Autobiography*,

> From his own intercourse with me I could derive none but a very humble opinion of myself... I was not at all aware that my attainments were anything unusual at my age... if I thought anything about myself, it was that I was rather backward in my studies, since I always found myself so, in comparison with what my father expected from me. (Mill, 1971, p. 35)

Leo Wiener, as we have seen, repeatedly emphasized that he regarded his son as an essentially average boy whose unusual abilities were the result of exceptional training. And Boris Sidis was adamant that William's remarkable early accomplishments were the inevitable outcome of the equally remarkable early education the boy had been given.

Of course, we cannot accept these accounts entirely at face value. Just as we previously found it necessary to treat with some scepticism the assertions made by parents anxious to convince themselves and others that the remarkable abilities of their offspring could only be attributed to miraculous powers, or divine selection, or parental genes, we need to be no less wary about accepting the equally confident opposing statements of those parents who have wanted all the world to appreciate the effectiveness of the training procedures they have devised, with their own children used as guinea pigs. The fact that those brothers and sisters of child prodigies who were not submitted by their parents to any unusually intensive early educational regime did *not* develop any abilities that were at all precocious or exceptional, despite being brought up by the same biological parents, and in the same family home, as siblings who were exceptionally brilliant child prodigies, provides some support for the assertion that the extraordinariness of child prodigies' early backgrounds does account, at least in part, for their remarkable early development. That conclusion gains additional support from the finding that in cases where a number of children in the same family have each received intense and prolonged early education from the parents – as in the Thomson, Berle, and Mozart families, for example, or, more recently, the Menuhins – more than one child has gained exceptional abilities.

From the interview findings obtained in the Chicago studies it is clear that the available evidence about contemporary child prodigies paints a similar picture. Many of these children talked and read fairly early. However, the majority of those of the children examined by the Chicago-based researchers who could safely be labelled as being prodigies by the end of childhood were not particularly exceptional when they were very young. It was not until after they had begun to receive considerable amounts of training or special encouragement from their parents (or another adult) that they started to display abilities that were strikingly advanced for children of their age. This tended to happen after, rather than before, these children had become unusually interested in an activity, and after they had begun to channel their energies in that particular direction. Typically, by this time the child had been encouraged to regard himself or herself as having already gained some degree of competence at his (or her) own special skill. Usually, it was not until after a degree of self-identification with a skilled activity or an area of knowledge had been achieved, and the child had acquired the habit of practising the activity frequently and enthusiastically, that really exceptional achievements began to be displayed.

For instance, Lauren Sosniak (1990) points out that among the young concert pianists whose childhoods she investigated, the majority did not show any unusual promise at the start of their training. Even after seven years of study and practice, when they began to play in local competitions, they were frequently far from being successful. Sosniak reports,

> We began our study with the question of how individuals were discovered and then helped to develop their talents; we found the reverse. The youngsters spent several years acquiring knowledge and developing skills and dispositions appropriate for their fields before they were 'discovered' as the most talented in their family or in their neighborhood and accorded the status of biggest fish in their small ponds. In turn, a discovery of this sort, by a parent or teacher, typically led to increased opportunities for development. (Sosniak, 1990)

Yet there are occasional reports of children who have made extraordinary progress at a very early age, sometimes even in the first six months of life. One report by H. B. Robinson describes a boy who began speaking when he was five months old. A month later he had a 50-word vocabulary. At 13 months he started to read. By the time his age was two years and three months he knew five languages and could read in three of them, and had a good understanding of basic arithmetic. Even more remarkable is a young boy named Adam, who was aged three and a half when David Feldman (1986) began to investigate his early life. By that time he had already learned to read and write, spoke several languages, studied mathematics and composed music for the guitar. According to his parents, Adam had begun to speak not only in words but in grammatically correct sentences at three months of age. The parents reported that Adam engaged in complex conversations by six months, and that by his first birthday he could read simple books.

A problem with most of these cases is that all the information we have comes from the parents, whose detachment and objectivity is questionable, and even in the case of the boy Feldman discusses, Feldman himself did not observe the child until he was three years of age. Feldman notes that Adam's home life was quite extraordinary in the extent to which it was deliberately arranged to cater to the needs of a young child. It was an exceptionally child-orientated environment, and the rooms were arranged to give Adam space to explore and experiment. His parents – a science professor and a psychotherapist – had hoped for a bright child who 'would approach learning with joy, spontaneity, and excitement' (Feldman, 1986, p. 35), and had decided well before Adam was born that they would do all they could to give careful attention to the child's intellectual, social, and emotional needs.

Adam's parents took their responsibilities towards him very seriously indeed. They spent a large proportion of their time with Adam. Feldman says that when he first visited their house he found that it was crammed full of Adam's toys, educational materials of many kinds, and large numbers of books. The parents seem to have done as much as was humanly possible to provide a stimulating and encouraging environment for their child. David Feldman, who was no newcomer to witnessing the often unusual family backgrounds of child prodigies, was taken aback by the parents' absolute dedication and their 'unending quest for stimulating and supportive environments' (Feldman, 1986, p. 36).

What should we make of a child like Adam? In his first year he was already quite exceptionally precocious, even if we allow for possible exaggeration by his justifiably proud parents, who clearly shared an intense emotional involvement in their child's remarkable early progress. As we have seen, Adam's early environment was also exceptional. It would be fascinating to know how Adam would have developed had his early background been quite ordinary. Unfortunately, of course, there is simply no way of telling. It would also be fascinating to know how another child – an adopted infant, perhaps – would have developed in the identical home environment provided by Adam's parents. Again, sadly, there is no way to know. Although there does exist a substantial research literature on the effects of adoption on young children's intelligence, there are no studies in which adoptive parents have shown a degree of intense dedication to a child's early progress that was remotely comparable to that demonstrated by Adam's parents.

It is frustratingly difficult to provide firm statements about the extent, frequency, or magnitude of intellectual precocity in the first years of life. Uncovering the causes is even more difficult. Even when it is clear that an infant has been remarkably precocious, it is generally impossible to disentangle, retrospectively, the possible influences. On the one hand there are environmental factors that help determine a child's earliest experiences. On the other hand there are other possible causes of exceptional early development, such as genetic ones. Ascertaining the causes is not helped by the fact that most of the available evidence is in the form of parental reports, often made years after the events they describe. There are inevitable questions about the objectivity of the data.

There exist various snippets of autobiographical data that, on first inspection, seem to provide confirmatory evidence of the spontaneous or 'natural' appearance of already formed skills in the first year or two of a child's life, apparently in the absence of any instruction being received by the child. For example, in his book *Frames of Mind*, Howard Gardner (1984) quotes Aaron Copland saying about composing, 'it is something that the composer happens to have been born to do'. Gardner also reports Saint Saens's statement that the process of composing is like an apple tree producing apples. He refers to a claim by Artur Rubinstein, the pianist, that as a child he would refuse to speak but was always willing to sing, and that, although nobody in his family had any interest in music, he quickly mastered the piano with very little effort. Gardner also quotes an unnamed composer as saying that he could never understand how anyone could have difficulty recognizing tones and deciphering musical patterns, because 'It's something I've been doing since the age of three at least' (Gardner, 1984, p. 121). Gardner also relates Stravinsky's story of how, at the age of two, he astonished his parents by skilfully imitating some local people whom he had heard singing on their way home from work.

Unfortunately, autobiographical reports of early childhood are notoriously unreliable. Even when a person genuinely and strongly believes that what is being remembered about events in early life is taken from an unadorned record of those events, as laid down in childhood, it is almost always the case that adults' childhood memories have suffered from substantial distortions over the intervening years. For that reason, however convinced someone may be that a clear and unconta-minated memory for early childhood events is being drawn upon, the wisest course is to assume that considerable alter-ations to the original record have taken place, albeit without any awareness on the part of the person concerned.

Do parental efforts to accelerate a child's early progress sometimes fail entirely?

Do some young children fail to be affected at all by the kinds of strenuous parental efforts that (as we have repeatedly seen in this chapter) are usually apparent whenever the home circumstances of a child prodigy have been examined? Up to now we have only encountered cases in which, whether or not the child eventually developed into a happy and fulfilled adult, the parents' efforts did at least have enough initial success to ensure that their child, at some stage, was unusu-ally precocious.

There may well have been many cases in which the parents, however dedicated and however skilled they were at teaching, were denied even that success. Yet the record is mute: one does not come across case-histories describing the failed attempts of parents who have striven, but with no success at all, to give their children a remarkable early start. Of course, the lack of evidence of such failures cannot be taken as proof that they have not occurred: in the absence of published findings there is no way of telling. People are understandably more likely to report on their successful than on their unsuccessful efforts. Even when reports are written, ones that describe positive findings are more likely to see publication than those describing interventions that have had no apparent effects. Unhappily, this issue belongs to the category of subjects which, as Stephen Jay Gould remarks, 'are invested with enormous social importance but blessed with very little reliable information' (Gould, 1984, p. 22).

Granted that trying to answer hypothetical questions can be a frustratingly unproductive enterprise, it is tempting to enquire why some parental efforts to stimulate their children's progress fail completely, assuming that it is safe to assume that this does sometimes happen. If it does, it would not necessarily be right to conclude that such failures indicate that a child is 'slow' or 'born dull', or reflect any simple limitation in ability to learn, or even a lack of 'cleverness' or intelligence. As I have mentioned earlier, many learning difficulties are caused not by limitations that are narrowly intellectual in form, but by features of temperament or cognitive style that happen to be incompatible with the demands of a particular learning task. For this reason, a failure is just as likely to be caused by a child's being impulsive or distractible, or the absence of a habit of reflecting on things, as by slowness or inadequacy of learning processes.

'Slow learning' is often given as the main cause of learning failures, but it may be instructive to repeat an experience described by one psychologist, Dennis Stott. He spent much of his life investigating the causes of children's learning difficulties. Stott was struck by the fact that when he examined a large number of children who had learning difficulties he never seemed to encounter a child who was 'just dull'. He found that,

> In every case that I examined there was a mixture of temperamental handicaps, emotional stresses arising from severe family anxieties, social disadvantages, erratic schooling, long-standing ill health, any of which would have been sufficient to account for the academic failure. So I asked the teachers... to pick out for me those whom they regarded as simply of low intelligence, without behavioural, emotional, social or health handicaps. They readily agreed, thinking they had plenty of them. When I

asked for the lists they told me rather apologetically that they could find fewer than they thought... In not one case did I have to conclude that the child must have been genetically dull. (Stott, 1974, p. 68)

So even if it does turn out that some parents' efforts to advance their children's progress are totally unsuccessful, we shall need to be very cautious about forming conclusions concerning the reasons for such failures. It would certainly be unwise to leap to the conclusion that numerous children are simply too dull or slow to profit from early stimulation.

Chapter 5
Geniuses

Geniuses are fascinating for all kinds of reasons, but a particularly beneficial consequence of knowing about them is that of extending our understanding of the causes of high achievements. Much can be learned from geniuses that is relevant to the lives and attainments of people who are not quite so extraordinary.

Many people think of geniuses as being a kind of race apart, who possess special powers that are largely mysterious. In fact, however, although it is true that geniuses are remarkable men and women, and their achievements are often dazzling, there are no convincing reasons for believing that the origins of the capabilities and accomplishments of geniuses are totally distinct from the underlying causes of ordinary individuals' achievements.

The impossibility of defining genius

What is a genius? In scientific psychology is often helpful to start by defining terms, and in the case of genius a precise definition would help us to specify who does or does not belong within the genius category. But it has not proved possible to agree on such a definition. Broadly speaking, the word refers to men and women who have created literary, artistic or scientific masterpieces of exceptional power or inventiveness, or who have produced ideas of great power and originality. That may sound somewhat vague, but unfortunately the word 'genius' resists a clearer and more precise specification. Yet it is definitely a necessary word, and also a valuable one, even if its indefinability makes 'genius' less than satisfactory as a scientific concept.

A particular difficulty that impedes arriving at a precise and universally agreed definition of genius becomes apparent once we consider the circumstances in which people decide to call someone a genius. At first glance, it might seem that calling a person a genius is a way of describing that individual, as is done when we call someone fat or thin, or tall or short, or intelligent. But there is a major difference. Applying a description like 'fat' or 'thin' begins with a measurable attribute, and the availability of the latter makes it possible for different people to be accurately labelled as being fat, thin, and so on. With genius, however, it is different, because there is no such measurable attribute of the person. What we are actually doing when we say that some person is a genius is not really a matter of *describing* that person in terms of their measurable *qualities*, but one of *acknowledging* the person as being someone who has produced certain rare *accomplishments*.

Calling someone a genius is more like stating that the person is a champion or a winner than it is like describing them as, say, fat or intelligent. As it happens, most geniuses are indeed highly intelligent (although there are a few individuals who have been widely regarded as being geniuses but who would not have scored very highly on an intelligence test). Of course, being a genius takes more than intelligence, and there are numerous men and women who gain extremely high scores on intelligence tests but never come near to making the kinds of achievements that lead to a person being regarded as a genius.

In common with terms like 'champion' or 'winner', the word 'genius' is more of an accolade than a description. The word is applied to someone on the basis of whatever that person *achieves*, not what they *are*. Although genius is far from being a new term, the modern meaning of it is comparatively recent. In the past, the idea of a person's genius designated a kind of an attending spirit, not unlike a poet's muse, that was at least partly external to the person.

Because we cannot straightforwardly define genius, there is no obvious way to decide whether a particular individual deserves to be called a genius or not. Nor can we produce a definitive list of geniuses. We can of course assert that someone who is very widely acknowledged to have been a genius, such as Newton or Mozart or Darwin or Einstein, definitely ought to be regarded as one. Many people would also insist that a variety of other men and women, including Archimedes, Plato, Copernicus, Galileo, Michelangelo, Bach, Beethoven, and Shakespeare, were definitely geniuses. However, once we look beyond the rather small number of individuals who are almost universally agreed to belong within the genius category, we encounter a much larger number of creative men and women who some people but not others would acknowledge as a having been a genius. How do we deal with them? If you believe that Charlotte Brontë was a genius but another person disagrees, how is it possible to decide which of you is right? Because the term genius is not really a description but more of an acknowledgement or accolade, there is no entirely satisfactory way of resolving that problem. And because there are variations in the degree to which different people value someone's achievements, there are bound to be disagreements about the membership of the genius category.

Varieties of genius

What do geniuses have in common? They all produce great creative achievements, of course, but in many other respects they seem remarkably diverse. Isaac Newton was often rude and disagreeable, whereas Charles Darwin was a kind and considerate man who rarely caused offence. Albert Einstein was usually outgoing, and always keen to discuss his work, and his friends rated him highly as an amateur violinist, but Michael Faraday guarded his privacy and was reluctant to talk about the problems he was working on until he had arrived at a solution.

Geniuses also differ greatly in their backgrounds. Charles Darwin's family was very wealthy, but Michael Faraday's was very poor, and he had to leave school when he was thirteen. Fortunately Faraday's helpful employer ensured that in his job as an apprentice bookbinder there were plenty of opportunities to read many of the books he came across. The young Mozart received intensive training from a very early age from his father, himself a musician and music teacher with great ambitions for his son. As we have seen, John Stuart Mill, the great nineteenth-century social and political thinker, was also educated by his father, James Mill, himself an impressive scholar, whose teaching was partly motivated by a desire to produce someone who would be capable of carrying on the father's own work. The younger Mill's acquaintances told him that he struck them rather forcibly as being what they termed a 'manufactured' scholar. As we observed in Chapter 4, it was a struggle for the young Mill to gain for himself a sense of direction and purpose that would match the mental capacities with which his father's education had equipped him.

Just a few geniuses have managed to educate themselves by their own largely unaided efforts. One such individual was George Stephenson, the great railway engineer. Stephenson, who played a huge part in making the possibility of steam locomotives into a practical reality, a development that revolutionised passenger travel as well as the transportation of goods, grew up in considerable poverty. As we have seen, he never went to school at all, and it was only when he was aged eighteen and employed as a colliery worker that he could afford to pay a local teacher to help him learn to read.

Qualities geniuses share

In certain respects, however, geniuses are often similar to one another. But some of the similarities are only superficial. Often, for instance, there is an appearance of fluency, and even effortlessness, but that apparent ease is only possible because of the enormous efforts that the person has made in the past. Thus Mozart was renowned for the speed at which he produced musical compositions, but he was only able to work so fast as he did because of the huge investment he had made through constant training and practice, over a period of many years. Contemporaries remarked on the intensity of his concentration on his work. They described him as having the capacity to focus all his attention on whatever he was engaged in.

One way in which geniuses are genuinely similar to one another is their capacity to work extremely hard. They almost all display a remarkable single-mindedness and a very strong commitment to their activities. Geniuses are very sure about what they want to do. They may be impeded by doubts and uncertainties, as was James Watt, the great engineer who created steam engines that were huge improvements on the inefficient early engines. All geniuses have a strong sense of direction.

Indeed, diligence is a virtually universal characteristic of geniuses. When the great English painter J.M.W.Turner was asked to reveal the secret of his success he gave a straight reply. He said, 'The only secret I have got is dammed hard work' (Hamilton, 1997, p. 128). Isaac Newton, asked how he discovered the law of universal gravitation, replied that he did so by thinking about it continuously. Charles Darwin attributed his success partly to a capacity to reflect for years on an unexplained problem. Other qualities that he regarded as having helped him considerably were sheer industry and determination: in Darwin these were combined with a capacity for careful and sustained observation. Einstein, likewise, felt that unusual amounts of curiosity, determination, and hard work were vital ingredients of his effectiveness. He too was capable of maintaining a ferocious concentration of the questions and problems that he was trying to solve, for lengthy periods of time.

Other activities tend to get neglected by geniuses. When Mozart was working on music he seemed to be completely unaware of anything else. Newton cheerfully admitted that when he was working on a problem all other concerns would be completely forgotten. Mealtimes would be ignored and any guests would be likely to be abandoned. All Newton's attention would be directed to the problems he was wrestling with. Einstein, too, could be completely oblivious to social niceties. He would forget to put his socks on in the morning, and he insisted that learning to drive a car was too difficult a task for him to master.

Although most geniuses are happy to admit to being extraordinarily curious and unusually single-minded and diligent, a number of them have emphatically denied being more intelligent than other people. John Stuart Mill, undoubtedly one of the most perceptive thinkers of all time, felt certain that he was not inherently more clever than the average person. Darwin, also, was utterly convinced that he was in no respect particularly quick or intelligent. Einstein insisted that it was his unusual curiosity rather than exceptional intelligence that accounted for his achievements.

Of course, the fact that geniuses themselves *think* that they are not innately clever does not mean that they are necessarily correct about that, but their view does deserve to be listened to. Although others have often assumed that geniuses find it easy to do what other people find difficult, geniuses themselves do not experience their work as being at all easy.

One quality that does distinguish genius from others is a capacity to keep persisting, however frustratingly difficult the mental labour happens to be. Newton was described by one of his contemporaries as having studied so hard that, if it was not for the fact that he got some relief from concentrating on his studies at the times he was engaged in the practicalities of undertaking experiments, he would have killed himself with studying. His doggedness at persisting in the face of difficulties was extreme. That is illustrated by the following account of the manner in which Newton would respond when he found himself unable to understand an especially difficult passage encountered when he was studying mathematics from Descartes's *Geometry*. Newton, we are told,

> read it by himself when he was got over 2 or 3 pages he could understand no farther than he began again and got 3 or 4 pages farther till be came to another difficult place, than he began again and advanced farther and continued doing so till he had made himself Master of the whole. (John Conduit, quoted in Westfall, 1980, p. 111)

In other words, Newton just kept persisting. He would go on trying, time and time again, until he finally mastered the passage that was causing difficulties. And all this learning was achieved entirely on his own, without, in Conduit's words 'having the least light or instruction from any body'.

The capacity to doggedly persist at arduous undertakings that we have observed in geniuses such as Newton is especially necessary during the lengthy period of training that all major achievers have to undergo. Although it has often been assumed that the process of acquiring the skills and knowledge that creative endeavours build upon is easier or quicker for geniuses than for other people, that is decidedly not the case. It takes a very substantial amount of time, and plenty of effort, for any person to master a difficult skill. Geniuses may spend just as long at this as anyone else, and like others they are helped by starting young. As the eighteenth-century British artist Reynolds observed,

> a facility of drawing, like that of playing upon a musical instrument, cannot be acquired but by an infinite number of acts... And be assured, that if this power is not acquired when you are young, there will be not time for it afterwards; at least the attempt will be attended with as much difficulty as those experience who learn to read and write after they have arrived at the age of maturity. (Hamilton, 1997, p. 23)

The necessity for training

All geniuses require a great deal of time to equip themselves with the capabilities their accomplishments draw upon. That is true even of someone like Mozart, even though he was clearly outstanding from a very early age. The fact that Mozart was already impressing audiences with his performing skills at the age of seven or so has led people to believe that his skills were gained effortlessly, but that is far from being the case. It is true that his capabilities as a child performer were very impressive, and yet a number of today's promising young musicians are even more accomplished. Mozart's musical education was extremely intensive. It started when he was very young, and would have filled as much as 20 000 or 30 000 hours, an immense period of time. Essentially, the young Mozart lived in a world of music, and musical activities took up a large proportion of his waking hours.

Of course, however uncommon Mozart's first experiences were and however intensive his training, it is hard to understand how he could have produced masterpieces of musical composition in early childhood, as he is supposed to have done. But here the real state of affairs is somewhat different from what is widely believed. Contrary to the myth that Mozart composed great masterworks at the age of four or five, one investigation has revealed that none of the compositions by him that are now regarded as being major works were actually written earlier than around the twelfth year of his musical career (Hayes, 1981). So it was only after many years of rigorous training to be a composer that he began to produce his greatest music. Like everyone else, Mozart needed a very long period of preparation in order to reach his peak.

A similar conclusion concerning the necessity to engage in lengthy training in order to become a composer emerged when Hayes submitted the musical output of 76 major composers to the same kind of analysis. The standard that was adopted for regarding a composition as being one that we now judge to be of major importance was that it should be sufficiently highly regarded nowadays for several recordings of it to be currently available. (Adopting this criterion is a sensible way of excluding items recorded only for their novelty value, or as disk fillers.) It turned out that only three of the 76 composers whose work Hayes studied had produced major works by the tenth year of their composing career. (The three are Satie, who produced 'Trois Gymnopédies' in his eighth year as a composer, and Shostakovich and Paganini, each of whom composed a notable masterwork after a mere nine preparatory years!)

The message of Hayes's findings is clear: all musical composers have to go through a very long period of learning their craft. There are no short cuts to musical greatness, not even for the most brilliant. Although popular accounts of remarkable individuals like Mozart may suggest otherwise, the belief that certain talented individuals are able to produce masterpieces without having to invest the years of careful preparation that other people require in order to reach high levels of expertise is simply mistaken.

The fact of the matter is that not only composers but all creators of outstanding human achievements, from artists and writers to scientists and mathematicians, reach the highest levels of competence only after many years of painstaking training. The most striking feats depend on skills that require thousands of hours of practice. Often, vast quantities of knowledge need to be gained as well. Chess masters, for instance, all have to acquire a capability to perceive the significance of numerous different chess positions. Their ability to recognize any of around 50 000 distinct patterns, each comprising several chess pieces (Simon and Chase, 1973) is only made possible by the fact that a vast array of knowledge will have been acquired in the course of years of training, during which something in the region of 20 000 hours is devoted to studying and playing the game. Consequently, even the most exceptional players of all take at least ten years of concentrated training to reach the highest levels of chess mastery.

Great writers, too, have to spend numerous hours gradually acquiring their expertise. In the case of the Brontë sisters, for example, the activity of writing filled much of their childhoods. They produced numerous stories, and while it is true that they would have perceived what they were doing as being recreation rather than study or work, it was only as a result of this lengthy informal training that they gained the capabilities that made it possible for them to become accomplished authors. Similarly, with other major writers such as Dickens and George Eliot, while they may not have consciously engaged in formal training in writing, they too devoted numerous hours to the kinds of writing activities that lead to the acquisition of impressive writing skills.

Creative activities

Just as the acquisition of the skills and capabilities a genius depends upon invariably demands large quantities of time and effort, so too do the actual creative activities that are more directly involved in the manufacture of masterpieces.

According to a common myth about geniuses, for a few special individuals the creative activities that lead to the production of exceptional creative achievements may be easy and fluent, and require no conscious effort at all. It would appear, according to this view, that some fortunate individuals do not experience the intense struggle that most people have to go through in order to create substantial achievements.

A number of reports, including some autobiographical ones, speak of effortless insights that occur quite spontaneously, in the arts and sciences alike. An especially well-known instance of the apparently 'unconscious' production of a masterpiece is described in Coleridge's account of the writing of 'Kubla Khan'. Another is Kekule's report of his discovery of the benzene ring. Both accounts seem to suggest that most, if not all, of the creative work must have been done while its author was sleeping. Kekule's discovery is said to have appeared to him in a vivid dream about snakes. Coleridge claimed that the poem appeared in his mind in a finished form on his awakening from a deep sleep. In the words of his own report, written in 1816, of events which took place in 1797,

> The Author continued for about three hours in a profound sleep, at least of the external senses, during which time he had the most vivid confidence, that he could not have composed less than from two to three hundred lines... On awakening he appeared to himself to have a distinct recollection of the whole, and taking his pen, ink, and paper, instantly and eagerly wrote down the lines that are here preserved. (Quoted by Perkins, 1981, p. 10)

But on closer examination the picture that emerges is not nearly so simple as that. To take the case of 'Kubla Khan', for example, it quickly becomes apparent that Coleridge's part in the production of the poem was not at all passive and far from being entirely spontaneous (Lowes, 1927; Perkins, 1981). Like a number of the Romantics, Coleridge combined an appetite for laborious work with an inclination to strike a pose of being capable of effortless masterpieces, even if that involved major departures from the literal truth (Howe, 1982). Coleridge's account of the writing of 'Kubla Khan' is partly untrue. Evidence that he engaged in editorial work on an early version proves that, his own story notwithstanding, the poem did not suddenly appear to him in its finished form. He drew upon a number of different sources, which supplied certain of the images and also some of the actual phrases that appear in the published poem.

And Kekule was almost certainly not actually dreaming when he made his discovery, although he may have been lost in thought about the scientific problem, which had been pre-occupying him over a long period of time (Perkins, 1981; Weisberg, 1986). In reality, the making of a masterpiece always involves a great deal of deliberate conscious effort. However, that is not to deny that we may be unaware of much of the mental work that our brains engage in.

Progress towards new discoveries is neither regular nor predictable. Ideas can take shape in sudden leaps of thought, with no prior warning, sometimes on awakening, or following a period of daydreaming or semi-sleep (Rothenberg, 1979). Mental activities that take place during periods of sleep or day-dreaming may often be crucial. But that does not mean that effort is unnecessary. No outstanding human achievement has ever been produced without a great deal of conscious work on its creator's part.

Inventions from scratch?

Just as mistaken as the idea that artistic or scientific achieve-ments can be created entirely unconsciously is the related view that great artists and scientists can make original contributions entirely on their own, from scratch, and without needing to draw on the experiences and achievements of their prede-cessors. Again, the reality is very different from that. All inven-tors and discoverers build on past achievements. Inventions rarely take the form of one huge leap from nowhere, and are much more likely to involve a number of advances, often made over a period of years by a number of different individuals.

Take the steam engine, for example. Many people believe that George Stephenson invented it. He did not, although he made extremely important contributions to the development of steam locomotives. Nor did James Watt, another great engineer to whom the invention of steam engines is often attributed. Steam engines built by an engineer named Thomas Newcomen were in use at the time Watt was born. Newcomen was proba-bly the first engineer to manufacture a practical steam engine with moving parts, but even he depended on earlier pioneers for discovering the underlying principles of steam power. As early as the seventeenth century, a man named Thomas Savery had taken out a patent for a device that used a vacuum produced by heating water in order to pump water out of mines, and around 1 500 years before that the Greek thinker Hero had designed a device that used steam to cause a wheel to revolve.

The real circumstances surrounding the invention of aeroplanes were not entirely dissimilar (Weisberg, 1993). Contrary to the myth that powered flight was discovered by the Wright brothers, suddenly and out of the blue following some brief experiments they conducted in periods of leisure from their daily work as bicycle mechanics, the true story is more complicated. At the time when the Wright brothers were active, there was considerable interest in the possibility of flying. The brothers had grown up in a home environment that gave them plenty of opportunities to learn about machines. When the older brother, Wilbur, was eleven, the boys had even been given a rubber-powered toy helicopter. By the time they reached adulthood scientific knowledge of aeronautics was growing fast, and the Wrights, who had very carefully studied the reports made by a number of other capable inventors who were attempting to produce flying machines, made sure that they had access to all the relevant information about the principles of flight that was becoming available. In 1896, one other inventor had succeeded in getting a steam-powered model to reach a height of 100 feet. Another inventor, who was experimenting with gliders, constructed one that stayed aloft for periods of around ten seconds, during which it travelled around 250 feet.

So the Wright brothers were definitely not starting from nowhere. Their inventions were not born in a vacuum. They were far from being ill-equipped or unprepared for their accomplishment. Their inventive work involved the efficient exploitation of knowledge and expertise that had been carefully acquired by themselves and others, over a lengthy period of time. Their work drew upon various kinds of data that other inventors had made available. And they went about their activities in a highly organised manner, making detailed plans and setting themselves intermediate targets that formed stepping stones leading in the direction of the goal of powered flight. There was plenty of rigorous planning and careful analysis, and much trial-and-error experimentation. The Wright brothers' eventual success only appears sudden or unexpected if one is ignorant of the lengthy efforts that preceded it. As in the case of the invention of steam engines, there was no single moment of discovery.

Breadth of interests

The fact that geniuses habitually specialize in their particular area of greatest concern, concentrating their efforts in a highly focused way, may seem to suggest that geniuses are narrow in their interests. But generally speaking that is not the case. Albert Einstein was a highly capable amateur violinist as well as being a great physicist, and George Eliot was a very good performer at the piano in addition to being a novelist of genius. And even in their work, the achievements made by geniuses often demand a number of different qualities, going beyond purely intellectual capacities.

Take the case of Darwin, for example. In the popular imagination he is perceived as a reclusive scientist who was preoccupied with his poor health and rarely left the house he inhabited for almost forty years. The real picture is very different. Darwin's great achievements were only possible because as well as having impressive intellectual capacities he was a socially accomplished individual: he was very good at getting on with others. That was important to him because he depended on the cooperation of others in many of his scientific activities. Darwin relied in various ways on a large number of friends and collaborators. His career also depended upon his ability to get on with a number of distinctly prickly individuals, ranging from his own father to Robert Fitzroy, the captain of H.M.S. *Beagle*, on which Darwin spent the five crucial years of its voyage round the world.

Conclusion

Geniuses are a very mixed bunch. In many ways they differ enormously from one another, but they all share certain key attributes. For example, all geniuses have a strong sense of direction and are immensely curious. Once committed to an activity, they persist at it doggedly, often to the exclusion of many of the interests and responsibilities that fill ordinary people's days. Although some of the creative activities of geniuses may seem effortless, an immense amount of effort, in the form of arduous training and rigorous preparation, will have gone into making those activities possible.

Chapter 6

Intelligence and high abilities

Highly able individuals are usually intelligent. They tend to gain high scores at the kinds of intelligence tests that assess a person's IQ, or intelligence quotient. But the relationship between specific abilities and general intelligence is not entirely straightforward. It is widely assumed that while abilities are essentially aquired and changeable, someone's IQ level is an inherent underlying quality of the person, at least partly innate and to a considerable extent fixed and unchanging. So while few teachers would raise any objection to the statement that a child did well at school because she was intelligent, the statement that a young person was intelligent because she did well at school would raise eyebrows. However, the view that general intelligence is more fundamental and less changeable than particular abilities can be challenged. It is not supported by firm evidence.

We begin this chapter by raising some practical questions concerning the value of intelligence tests for *predicting* human abilities. To what extent do IQ scores provide useful information about the likelihood of a person succeeding at difficult tasks? And how good are intelligence tests for selecting potentially high achievers? Afterwards we turn to some queries about the role of the concept of intelligence in *explaining* abilities.

Intelligence tests as predictors of accomplishments

Current tests of intelligence have evolved from ones that were constructed by Alfred Binet at the beginning of the twentieth century for a highly practical purpose. A device was needed that would help to identify schoolchildren who lacked abilities needed for benefiting from the classroom teaching that was offered in (French) schools. Sensibly, the choice of items was made on the basis of their capacity to assess some of the same skills and abilities as were necessary for succeeding at classroom learning. With that in mind, some of the items initially chosen were ones that had been suggested by teachers.

Since the original tests were first devised there have been many changes, and intelligence testing has become a highly sophisticated commercial enterprise. However, the changes that have been made over the years have generally been minor ones. That is partly because one of the criteria adopted for selecting new or revised items has been their effectiveness at yielding patterns of scores similar to those produced by tests comprising the items already in use.

How effective are the tests? That partly depends upon what they are being used for. Intelligence test scores do enable tolerably accurate predictions to be made concerning how well a child will do at school. The tests are also useful to a limited extent for predicting how adults will perform at problems that are broadly similar to ones encountered in schools. But intelligence tests are less effective for predicting someone's performance at practical and everyday tasks, even intellectual ones, that are encountered outside educational institutions.

The only major exceptions to that generalization occur when the achievement of a certain degree of educational success is used by those who regulate jobs or professions as a necessary credential for entry. In these instances educational achievement (which is fairly closely related to measured intelligence) forms a hurdle or barrier that has to be overcome in order for someone to qualify for opportunities for advancement, or have access to training. That can lead to unfair discrimination against individuals who may possess all the mental skills necessary for success but who happen not to have the kind of educational and social background associated with high levels of performance on intelligence tests (Howe, 1997).

The majority of skills needed in order to do well at jobs in the real world are only rather weakly related to the mental capabilities that are assessed in intelligence tests (Weinert and

Waldmann, 1986). Even authorities who take a favourable view of intelligence testing concede that correlations between IQ and indicators of success at jobs are low, ranging from around .2 and .6.

What does that mean in practice? Taking the average correlation as being .4, that implies that the proportion of the variability in people's job performance that is accounted for by the differences between individuals in their tests scores is only 16. per cent (that is, the .4 correlation, squared).

The fact that entry requirements are often based on educational achievements can artificially inflate the magnitude of relationships between intelligence-test performance and success in non-school areas of achievement. When that source of distortion is removed, correlations between a person's test scores and the same individual's success at skills required at work and in other contexts of everyday life tend to be very low, and sometimes zero. When positive correlations do still remain after corrections have been made to remove the above source of distortion, they are rarely sufficiently large to account for much above 15 per cent of the variability between individuals in their level of performance at job or everyday skills. Even that limited contribution can be useful, however, if it is necessary to select a large number of individuals for positions that demand a degree of mental ability, and if no other information about the candidates' capabilities is available.

Some researchers argue that even without making adjustments to compensate for the confounding influence of amount of schooling, correlations between tested intelligence and job effectiveness are more modest than the figure of .4 indicated above, and are typically nearer .2 (McClelland, 1973). Correlations of this magnitude are too low to be of any practical help for making accurate predictions about individuals' chances of vocational success. (A correlation of .2 between IQ scores and job performance measures implies that differences in test scores account for only 4 per cent of the variability between people in their job performance.) Klemp and McClelland (1986), who carefully watched senior managers actually performing their work, concluded that the intellectual abilities required for managerial success are very different from the skills that intelligence tests measure.

Intellectual abilities are also required by people doing non-managerial jobs. For instance, employees as diverse as warehouse workers, product assemblers, and delivery drivers all make use of a variety of intricate mental strategies. But these, too, are largely unrelated to intelligence test scores (Scribner, 1986). The same is true of the abilities needed for adjustment to military life (Zigler and Seitz, 1982).

A further limitation is that even when IQ scores do provide some benefit in helping to predict job success, that may only be true for the first few months that a person holds the job. By the time someone has been doing a job for a longer period, the correlation between success at the job and IQ score is likely to reduce, sometimes to zero. In some instances it has been found that after working at the same job for some years, those employees with lower IQ scores were outperforming those with higher intelligence test scores (Kamin, 1995).

At first glance, IQ scores seem to be good predictors of economic and social success. Correlations between a man's childhood IQ and his wealth and success as an adult are as high as .8 in some investigations. Other studies have found lower correlations, in the region of .5, between IQ in adolescence and occupational status in late adulthood (Rutter, 1989).

Does the fact that these correlations exist mean that IQ level is a cause of a person being successful? It seems not, because the correlations have been found to be largely a side-effect of influences such as schooling and family background that can affect both IQ scores and vocational success. The reason for concluding that a person's family background is more influential than the individual's IQ is that studies have shown that the effects of family background on a person's success when IQ is held constant are much more substantial than the effects of IQ differences when family background is held constant.

For example, among men who all have average IQs, those from the highest socioeconomic classes are more than seven times more likely to receive high incomes than men from the poorest families. Also, men having average IQs whose years of schooling are exceeded by no more than 10 per cent of the population are over ten times as likely to be in the highest income group as men who are in the lowest 10 per cent of the population in the number of years of schooling they have received.

These findings show that the observation that test scores may help predict a person's success in life does not necesarily indicate that high IQ is a necessity. A more likely explanation is that the IQ scores happen to be correlated with other factors, such as parental wealth, that are genuinely influential. Stephen Ceci and Charles Henderson discovered that the variables that are strong predictors of adult income are the number of years of schooling and the social background of the family (Ceci, 1990). Some research indicates that when schooling and socioeconomic background are held constant, the proportion of the variation between people that is predicted by variations in IQ becomes negligible (Lewontin, 1982).

In other words, the predictive value of IQ scores as such, when schooling and social class are controlled, is considerably less than the predictive value of the other two, when IQ is controlled. As it happens, there are other attributes which are only weakly related to IQ but which are considerably better predictors of adult success than IQ scores. One is childhood temperament. Another is competence at making sensible plans during late adolescence (Rutter, 1989).

Intelligence tests and superior abilities

How effective are intelligence tests for making predictions that can aid selection processes involving highly able people? Can such tests predict which individuals among a number of highly capable people will produce the most exceptional achievements? On the whole, intelligence tests have a rather poor record here. One investigator, James Flynn, who examined the fortunes of Chinese immigrants to the United States after World War Two, discovered that while their IQ scores were below average, their actual achievements, relating to real life success, were well above average. For example, almost twice as many of these individuals, compared with native-born Americans, gained progressional occupational status. So it clearly cannot be assumed that IQ scores will invariably be good indicators of achievement levels.

One study that did appear to demonstrate that intelligence testing can be highly effective for identifying children who in adulthood would become very high achievers was initiated in California, early in the twentieth century, by Lewis Terman. His research team identified a large sample of 1500 children who scored well at intelligence tests, and they followed the children's progress throughout their lives. The IQs averaged around 150.

Many of the initial findings appeared to confirm that IQ scores are highly useful for identifying children who would be high achievers later on. For instance, the children Terman selected turned out to do well at school, at sports as well as academic subjects, and their physical health was also above average. And after they left school they went on doing well. More than ten times as many of them than the national average gained a university degree. They found better-than-average jobs, which were usually well paid. A substantial proportion of these people acquired jobs in the professions or became scientists or writers or business executives. Compared with the average individual they were also happier, and they even lived longer.

However, when comparisons were made between individuals differing in IQ *within* the sample collected by Terman and his team, the IQ scores failed to yield useful predictions. For example, in one of Lewis Terman's investigations he compared the 150 most successful and the 150 least successful of his intellectually gifted participants (Renzulli, 1986). Contrary to his expectations, Terman found that the two groups did not differ in measured intelligence. In other words, differences in their test scores were not among the causes contributing to the two groups' differing degrees of success.

Other factors were more important, and the particular traits on which the two groups were most distinct were not intellectual ones at all. Characteristics of personality and temperament were especially crucial, such as persistence in the accomplishment of ends, integration towards goals, self-confidence, and freedom from feelings of inferiority. Essentially, the reasons underlying the greater success of the individuals in one group, compared with the other group, lay in their greater drive to achieve and their better emotional and social adjustment.

Family background was a particularly crucial contributing influence. Between the least and most successful of the participants in Terman's study were large differences in the lifestyles of their families. As we found in Chapter 2, families are influential in many ways, and even when children from different kinds of families are similar in their IQs they are subject to contrasting kinds of influential experiences. Many of the experiences and opportunities available to a child depend largely upon the particular family background in which the young person grows up. So too do the role models a child has access to and the expectations of parents and other influential adults concerning the child's future progress.

The ways in which different kinds of families are effective at providing support systems for a child vary considerably. Prosperous families have access to social networks that can help a young person to get ahead. Such families are also likely to possess various kinds of useful know-how about how to get on in the world. Consequently, the extent to which a child comes to possess self-confidence and an expectation to do well may be greatly affected by family circumstances. In short, there are numerous cultural differences in the kinds of backgrounds that families provide, and these can profoundly affect the likelihood of a child prospering in adult life.

These findings seem to contradict the assertertions that Terman spent much of his life persuading people to accept, concerning the underlying importance of the qualities that are assessed by an intelligence test. Worse still, the apparent confirmation of the predictive value of IQ scores that was provided by Terman's conclusion (that the children identified as being intelligent in his California study did particularly well in adulthood) proved illusory. It turned out that the sample of children he initially identified as being superior, partly on the basis of their intelligence test scores, were actually no more successful in their later lives than a sample individuals chosen at random from children with similar family backgrounds would have been (Sorokin, 1956; Ceci, 1990). Also, in addition to the embarassing finding that intelligence scores obtained in childhood did not add to the accuracy of predictions concerning which of the individuals within the sample selected in the California study would be most successful in later life, it also emerged that those of the chosen individuals who were eventually the least successful did not differ at all from the others in their average childhood IQ scores (Howe, 1982; Elder, 1988; Elder *et al.*, 1989).

In conclusion, while it is true that intelligence test scores can be useful, they are very far from being accurate predictors of the kinds of skills and achievements that are important in real life. And such tests are especially ineffective at making predictions that concern the achievements of individuals who are particularly able. They do not distinguish between the highly able and the exceptionally able, so far as real life achievements are concerned. As aids in the process of selecting individuals who are likely to gain high abilities, intelligence tests are not very effective.

It is important to be aware of the limitations in the predictive value of intelligence tests, because otherwise we may err by attaching too much importance to test scores. That can easily happen. For instance, in a number of evaluations of the effectiveness of a number of Head Start compensatory education programmes in the United States, gains in IQ scores were perceived as a major indicator of the programmes' success (Lazar *et al.*, 1982; Ramey *et al.*, 1985). This perception had a number of negative consequences. For instance, it almost certainly resulted in insufficient attention being paid to the effectiveness of the programmes at achieving genuinely useful outcomes. Using IQ scores as a basis for assessing the extent to which an intervention increases the skills that children really do need is like having a plan to increase the output of a coal mine evaluated with a rating scale that was designed to measure the productivity of shipping companies. In both cases, the outcome is that the qualities that are actually being assessed are, at best, not the ones that it is most important to know about, and, at worse, largely irrelevant to the real aims.

Intelligence as an explanation

When someone attempts an intelligence test, that person's test scores are an indication of how well he or she has performed at a range of problems that draw upon various mental skills. So a person who scores well can be said to possess better mental skills, or more highly developed ones, than somone who scores poorly, at least so far as those particular capacities that the test questions draw upon are concerned. And since a person's score reflects that individual's performance at problems drawing upon a fairly wide variety of mental skills, it is hardly surprising to discover that the IQ score may be a moderately useful predictor of the same person's performance in other circumstances that demand mental competence.

Seen in that way, intelligence and intelligence testing are purely practical devices, concerned with assessments of a person's test performance and the possible practical uses of those assessments. Nothing is being implied about the underlying *reasons* for one person having better mental skills than another. There is no suggestion that any kind of deep explanation is being intended when it is noted that one person is more intelligent than another. Saying that someone is intelligent is simply a way of *describing* the person as someone who performs well, and possesses mental skills. It is not a way of *explaining why* that person does well, nor of accounting for how one man or woman came to have mental skills not possessed by another person.

However, many people have insisted that intelligence is more than simply a descriptive concept, in the sense indicated above. They claim that it is also an explanatory one. That is, they would insist by stating that one person is more intelligent than someone else one is also saying *why* the first person does better. The first person performs better, according to this view, *because* he or she is more intelligent: high intelligence *accounts for* superior peformance. As a *consequence* of the first person possessing more intelligence, he or she is more successful than the other individual.

Applied in this way, it is clear that the concept of intelligence can be seen to have a meaning for at least some of the people who introduce that term which goes well beyond being simply descriptive. Intelligence is being regarded as some underlying quality of the person. What is more, it is seen as a quality that makes it possible for them to perform various tasks that cannot be performed by people who lack that quality. Hence an intelligent person is someone who is not just smart, but someone who possesses some underlying capacity or quality that makes them smart. And the more of this quality a person has, the better, because that underlying quality of intelligence is what causes a person to be intelligent.

Is it or is it not legitimate to introduce the term intelligence with this explanatory sense in mind? Is it reasonable to regard intelligence as being an underlying quality that makes it possible for a person to act intelligently, rather than just being a word for describing the state of being intelligent?

Almost from the first time that intelligence test were first devised some of the psychologists involved in their production became convinced that intelligence tests were indeed measures of an underlying human quality, one that accounted for individual differences in people's capacity to solve mental problems. Even today, many if not most people who introduce the word 'intelligence' in psychology appear to believe, at least implicitly, that indicators of someone's intelligence level can help to explain the person's abilities.

Although few psychologists would admit to regarding intelligence as a concrete or tangible thing, many of the ways in which the term is introduced imply a belief by the user that the concept of intelligence is more than just a descriptive construct. For example, psychologists and educators frequently describe intelligence as being central to, or giving rise to, or being necessary for, or the cause of, or at the root of or the heart of, or basic or fundamental to specific abilities, or as 'underlying' them. Alternatively, people often say that certain skills 'depend upon' or 'require' or 'demand' a degree of intelligence. The use of any of these words or phrases carries with it the implication that intelligence functions as a cause, and hence an explanation, of certain abilities that are present in a person.

Is the concept of intelligence a genuinely explanatory one, or not? A possible response, if a naïve one, is to say that the very question is absurd. Common sense tells us that intelligence is something real, and a quality that plays a fundamental role in determining what we can do. Of course the concept of intelligence is one that explains things, according to that view.

But commonsense assumptions can be wrong, and words can mislead. It is easy to make the error of 'reifying' words and concepts. People make that error as a consequence of assuming that wherever there is a word there must also be some concrete thing that the word refers to. Such an error in a person's thinking can easily lead to someone assuming that the mere existence of the word intelligence provides grounds for inferring that an underlying thing or quality of intelligence must also exist.

Especially with a common word like intelligence, the very familiarity of the term may make it especially difficult to detect that there is a possible reification error involved. The fact that intelligence is a word we often use in our non-scientific, everyday psychological thinking adds to the difficulty of being entirely rational about it, by making intelligence something very real for most people. The fact that intelligence refers to qualities that have an important place in people's feelings about themselves can add to the difficulty of straight thinking about that concept.

As well as falling into the error of reifying, people can easily fail to make the necessary distinction between descriptive and explanatory concepts. It is often wrongly assumed that a word which describes something will also explain it. Also, we may fail to recognize that a strong conviction that something exists compensates for a lack of evidence that it actually does. So it is not impossible that the firm view shared by numerous people that intelligence must exist as a real underlying personal quality could eventually turn out to be comparable to the convictions of those millions of individuals throughout the ages who have been certain of the powers of stone idols or evil spirits, or the scientists in the past who were certain of the existence of phlogiston, or firmly believed that people's temperaments depended on the four humours.

With concepts that are psychological, as intelligence is, distinguishing between between ones that are genuinely explanatory and ones that are merely descriptive can be especially difficult. With non-psychological concepts it is often easy to make this distinction and notice when a concept is being wrongly used. For instance, if descriptive words such as 'productive' or 'successful' appear in contexts that indicate that an explanation is being intended, as in

My factory produces more goods than yours because it is more productive, or

> She is doing well because she is successful,

or

> My car goes faster than yours because it is speedier,

it is fairly clear that something is wrong. Despite the presence of the word 'because' nothing is really being explained. The circularity of what is being expressed is transparent: it is easy to see that there is a kind of verbal sleight of hand. But with a sentence such as

> He found the problem easy because he is intelligent,

the assumption that something is being explained would usually go unquestioned. It is implicitly assumed that the word 'intelligent', unlike 'productive' and 'successful ', can serve the function of explaining things as well as describing. People are often not even aware of the possibility that the word 'intelligence' is really no more than descriptive, indicating what someone can do but not genuinely explaining why that person can do it.

However, it remains possible that the concept of intelligence is a genuinely explanatory one, after all. My main purpose here is simply to draw attention to the tendency of users of the word to make the assumption that it must be, in the absence of any evidence that it actually is. But, if the construct of intelligence is to play a role in attempts to explain human abilities, it is essential to begin by establishing that it can do more than just describe. Otherwise, saying 'she did well because she is intelligent' would only be equivalent to saying that the person succeeded because she is the kind of person who does well. In other words, what appears to be an explanation would be simple a rephrasing, like Molière's remark that a sleeping potion makes people sleep because of its dormative properties, or the comment that a person failed at something 'because he was a loser' (Olson, 1986; see also Stott, 1974; Keating, 1984; Bynner and Romney, 1986; Horn, 1986; Howe, 1988a; 1988b; 1989b).

A general factor

All that we know for certain is that some people perform better than others at solving various mental challenges, including the ones incorporated in intelligence tests. It is certainly conceivable that the reason for this is that there exists some underlying quality of the brain that people in the former group possess to a greater degree than people in the latter group. That such underlying quality of intelligence does indeed exist has been insisted upon very forcefully by a number of experts on intelligence, starting with Charles Spearman at the beginning of the twentieth century.

Various findings have been cited as providing evidence for the existence of intelligence as the underlying quality. One is the fact that scores at the different groups of items making up an intelligence test tend to correlate, with the patterns of correlations making it possible for what is known as a 'general factor' of intelligence to be extracted from the measures of performance, by means of various algebraic calculations. The presence of this factor, usually referred to as g, has been taken by some as forming evidence that there is 'something in common' to people's performances at different test items, and, by implication, to underlying mental capacities.

Other findings that have been thought to provide evidence of a general underlying quality of intelligence take the form of correlations that have been found between intelligence test performance, on the one hand, and, on the other, performance at very simple tasks that have been thought to provide indicators of the underlying speed of a person's mental processing. It has been claimed that these findings establish that differences between people in their intelligence test scores are related to fundamental differences between individuals in the speed at which their brains are capable of processing information.

However, there are alternative possible explanations for these findings. The fact that there are correlations in people's performance levels at various intelligence test items is certainly not proof of the existence of some single underlying process. One possible reason is that any two different items may draw upon mental skills that are common to both items. Another reason is that with some pairs of items a person may possess knowledge that can contribute to the solution of both of them. A third reason is that there are various characteristics of the person that will have a similar influence upon performance at two test items, or upon performance at a test item and the same person's at a task that is intended to measure some kind of basic capacity or mental processing time, even if the different tasks involved have no elements in common. Such personal characteristics include self-confidence, enthusiasm, dogged-ness and persistance, and attentiveness. Also, if a person happens to be especially alert at a particular time, or especially bored, or fatigued, that state of mind may well exert a similar influence on performance at various test items, even when those items have nothing at all in common.

In short, the fact that various correlations can be discovered in relation to different indicators of mental performance is far from being sufficient grounds for deducing that there exists some underlying quality of intelligence that contributes to all of the tasks involved. There are plenty of other possible contributing reasons for the presence of the correlations. In the circumstances, it would be very surprising if no correlations in test-item performance were encountered: the fact that they are found is readily explained.

So the question of whether or not there does exist some single underlying quality of intelligence remains controversial. It is entirely possible – and in my view most likely – that numerous different causes contribute to the fact that one person is more intelligent than another, and that the belief that there is some single underlying cause is quite wrong. Reality is far more complicated than that. There are many different reasons for people differing in their abilities, and in the scores that they gain at intelligence tests.

Chapter 7

Innate talents: reality or myth?

In previous chapters, I have drawn attention to numerous influences that can contribute to high abilities, but the emphasis has been on those causes that exert their effects through a person's experiences. These causes include various kinds of learning, formal and informal, deliberate and incidental. Another group of influences on abilities has been given less attention. These have their origins in biological sources of individual variability. Such biological differences between people often stem from inherited characteristics, and are essentially innate, even though their effects may not be evident until well after a person's birth.

The talent account and its implications

I discussed, in Chapter 1, the widespread belief that differences between people that take the form of innate gifts and talents play a crucial role in making high abilities possible. The absence of such talents is thought to rule out the chances of some individuals excelling in certain areas of skill. Conversely, their presence is thought to make success possible, and perhaps probable, in the favoured minority of people who happen to be born with a talent to excel at the skill in question.

In that discussion, which is continued in the present chapter, I was somewhat critical of the notion of an innate gift or talent. It is true that there are certain phenomena, including some remarkable capabilities seen in a few individuals, that appear at first to be explicable in no other way. On closer examination, however, it is clear that alternative explanations are possible after all.

I also argued that so long as the question of whether or not innate talents form a major influence on human abilities remains undecided, it may be wise to make the working assumption that they do not exist, rather than to assume that they do. My reason for taking that stance arises from the fact that there are adverse consequences of influential adults, such as teachers and parents, believing in the existence of such innate gifts as crucial influences. The policies that are based on that belief lead to numerous young people being deprived of the opportunities and training facilities that are necessary for a person to reach the highest levels of expertise in a complex and difficult field of competence. That happens because if a child is thought to lack a talent, the necessary training is likely to be denied to that child, simply because of adults' assumption that the lack of talent will make it impossible for that young person to take proper advantage of that training.

If the belief in gifts and talents turns out to be well based, the denial of opportunities to individuals lacking such gifts can be seen as justifiable, of course. It makes sense to target scarce training resources towards those young people who can take best advantage of them and away from those who cannot. However, if it is eventually established that innate talents and gifts are actually fictitious entities, denying opportunities to those deemed to lack them would amount to unfair and entirely unjustifiable discrimination against the many individuals who are not chosen.

No such unfair discrimination could follow from making the alternative working assumption, namely that innate talents and gifts do not exist. Consequently, even if it was to be subsequently discovered that such an assumption is incorrect, that mistake – unlike the alternative one – would not have caused harm. It would not create the unfair discrimination that is an almost inevitable consequence of adults making choices under the influence of an erroneous belief in the influence of innate gifts and talents.

An important distinction

It is clearly important to verify the truth or falsity of the innate talent account. Also, however, it is just as necessary to appreciate that there is an important distinction to be drawn here. That is, there is a big difference between the broader question of whether innate biological differences between people can affect their abilities and the more specific question of whether or not there exist innate causes of varying abilities in the particular form of gifts and talents. A consequence of this distinction is that the finding that biological differences are an important influence would not by any means justify the inference that the innate talent account must be correct.

Inherited differences between people may influence their eventual characteristics, including their capabilities, in ways that are direct or indirect, and predictable or unpredictable. Just as a storm in Thailand may have an influence (albeit a very indirect one) upon the weather in Australia, but may do so in a manner that, for all practical purposes, nobody could possibly have predicted in advance, it is equally possible that a genetically caused difference between two individuals could have an effect that eventually contributes to the differing capabilities of the two people.

However, indirect influences of that kind, despite the evidence of biological involvement, would lack some essential attributes of innate gifts and talents. What people mean by these latter terms is fairly specific. Talents are seen as more than just vague innate qualities that have unpredictable effects upon a person. On the contrary, gifts and talents are supposed to have reliable and predictable influences: they can be detected in an individual at an early age, well before the full flowering of the special capability that the presence of the innate gift or talent is believed to make possible.

In other words, talents and gifts are assumed by those who make important practical decisions that are based upon a belief in their existence to be, first, identifiable at an early age, and, second, to provide a justification for making predictions concerning future events. When teachers or trainers select certain young people because they think that they possess innate talents necessary for success, they are explicitly or implicitly making these two assumptions about the ways in which talents work.

Because the specific question of the existence of talents is distinct from the broader issue of the possible roles of biologically based differences between individuals, I shall look at the two matters separately, taking the broader issue first.

Innate differences and their possible effects on abilities

A common misconception about the manner in which people are differently affected by variability stemming from differences in the biological characteristics individuals inherit is that complex human attributes are straightforwardly regulated by particular genes. Every so often newspapers announce the discovery of a gene for this or a gene for that, such as language, reading, determination, obesity or musical ability. An implication is that single genes can be identified that determine the form and magnitude of these qualities in individuals.

In fact, genes do not operate in a way that is remotely like that, at least in the case of complex human traits. The very word 'gene' is itself an abstraction: physical analysis of the DNA material that conveys genetic information does not reveal identifiable units that correspond with the idea of a single gene. And the popular view of genes as blueprints or instructions that form complete recipes for creating organisms in the image of their forebears is a gross oversimplification.

It would be more realistic to think in terms of various kinds of information-bearing genetic material. This can be utilised in various ways at any of a number of stages. It thereby contributes, in conjunction with other influences, to the design and manufacture of organisms. Importantly, the actual relationship between an item of genetic material and some characteristic that may be affected by it can be remote and far from direct, as well as being unpredictable.

Take a trait such as intelligence, for instance. It is conceivable that there are many thousands of items of genetic information that are capable of having effects that may, perhaps at some point in a long chain of intervening influences, affect a person's activities in ways that have an influence upon that individual's intelligence. Sometimes genetic information may help initiate a chain of events: on other occasions genetic information may make an input at a later stage. Importantly, however, the fact that there is genetic involvement does not mean that it is possible to identify items of genetic material that can be reliably expected to exert this or that specific influence on a person's intelligence.

The roles of genetic materials

Rather than imagining that a gene is something that has an influence that directly affects a complex psychological characteristic, it is more accurate to think of the immediate effect of genetic information being to influence, say, the production of some or other hormone. Genes are actually sequences of DNA base pairs that contribute to the manufacture of proteins. They do that by affecting the structure of amino-acid sequences. Depending on the circumstances, this activity can influence occurrences at a future stage. Eventually, following what may be a very lengthy chain of actions, there may be consequences that affect an individual's psychological capabilities.

However, at each of a number of stages the actual effects of a particular item of genetic information will depend on other factors. Because of that, the long-term influences of genetic materials will be largely unpredictable. So even when it is indisputable that genetically based sources of human variability have been contributing influences on the development of individual people, it would be wrong to conclude that those qualities that have been affected by genetic materials have been straightforwardly determined by them.

In practice, it may be impossible to predict in advance the eventual consequences of a particular difference in the genetic materials possessed by two individuals. Partly for that reason, the belief that at some future stage it may be possible to 'read' the genetic information in the cells of a newborn baby and make accurate predictions about that individual's later achievements is an unrealistic one.

It should now be apparent that the ideas about genetic causation that are evoked by newspaper accounts of the search of 'the' gene for intelligence, or any other psychological quality, are misguided. Such accounts are not compatible with a realistic knowledge of the manner in which genetic information actually contributes. There is no simple or direct relationship between an individual's genetic make-up and that person's psychological characteristics.

Nevertheless, statements about 'the' gene for this or that continue to be made. One reason for the fact that they often go uncriticized is that they appear to be endorsed by the findings of research investigations in which certain gene abnormalities or malfunctions are demonstrated to have predictable effects. So a single gene can cause something to stop working properly. However, it should be noted that these reports invariably refer to circumstances in which certain genetic defects are reliably associated with particular malfunctions.

It is quite true that there are clear outcomes of genetic materials being missing or defective. That leads to malfunctions for much the same reason as a defective sparking plug can bring a vehicle to a halt or a loose connection cause a large computer to stop working. There are many circumstances in which a single broken link in a chain can paralyse a whole system.

But the fact that a defect in a single gene may lead to a breakdown does not mean that the same gene, when operating normally, is solely responsible for the activities to which it contributes. A single gene cannot make a person intelligent or more thoughtful, any more than a single connection can make my computer more powerful or a sparking plug control the operation of my car. The error underlying the belief that a single gene can be responsible for a complex quality such as human intelligence is illustrated by Stephen Pinker's citing of a politician's remark that 'Any jackass can kick down a barn, but it takes a carpenter to build one' (Pinker, 1997, p. 34–5).

Can genetic effects be measured?

Genetic differences between people are almost certainly among the influences that contribute to people differing in their abilities. Understandably, psychologists have sought to quantify the actual effects of genetic differences. However, apart from the unpredictability of some of the influences of variability in genetic materials, there are other difficulties, and there have been various misunderstandings about the effects of inheritance on human capacities. Contrary to common belief, with a few exceptions, human traits are not fixed by a person's genes. Even a person's body shape and rate of metabolism are partly determined by the environment (Lewontin, 1982). So if one member of a pair of identical twins lives at sea level and does light work while the other twin has a life working in the mountains as a heavy labourer, the two will develop very different body shapes and metabolic rates.

Second, as is also noted by Lewontin (1982), the apparently reasonable view that, although the environment has important effects, genes do place firm limits on capacities, is incorrect. Certain seemingly plausible metaphors admittedly seem to lend credence to that view. For instance, children's mental capacities have been compared to buckets which can be more or less full (depending on environmental factors) but whose total contents cannot exceed the limitations imposed by the size of the bucket. But in reality, different genotypes, unlike buckets, do not have different fixed capacities. Moreover, there is no ideal environment for each and every genotype. The environment that maximizes the growth of an organism of one genotype will not be the most favourable environment for a genetically different organism.

Third, geneticists insist that it is not even correct to assert that someone has a genetic tendency to exhibit a particular trait. By way of illustration, Lewontin points out that the statement that a person has a genetic tendency to be fat implies that in normal environments that person will be fatter than a person with no such genetic tendency. But this begs the question of what kinds of human environments are 'normal' ones. In practice this may be impossible to specify. Lewontin questions whether there is any basis for saying, for instance, that high or low levels of nutrition are more normal in human life, or the presence or absence of parasites, or individual competitiveness rather than collective sharing. Not only is it true that a person who 'tends to be fat' when there is a high level of nutrition will tend to be considerably thinner when the nutritive input is lower, it is also true that between a pair of people, the one who is thinner than the other when both of them consume a large amount of food may be fatter than the other when the amount each consumes is low.

Similar complications are encountered with respect to the differences in people's abilities. The individual who, after being subjected to one set of environmental circumstances performs better at a test than another person who has experienced the identical environment (so far as that is possible) may do worse than the second person if the two of them share a different environment. There are many situations in which a particular inherited characteristic may lead to a person doing better than someone else in certain environmental circumstances, but worse than that person in other circumstances.

Despite all these complexities, which can make it virtually impossible to know how differences between people in their genetic endowments will affect their capabilities, it is often assumed that we can discover whether inherited differences between individuals are more or less crucial, as influences on general intelligence and specific abilities, than differences in people's experiences of life. At least in principle, it ought to be possible for investigations using identical twins to compare the degree to which variations in mental capacities depend upon the effects of people's genetic differences with the degree to which they are affected by raising individuals in differing environments.

However, such a comparison is only possible if the identical twins participating in the investigation have really not shared environments at all. In practice, however, that is extremely difficult to guarantee. To be absolutely certain that two twins do not share any experiences it would be necessary to separate them soon after conception, but that cannot be done. The closest practical alternative is to locate twins separated at birth. But even that is almost impossible.

There are a number of reasons. First, only very unusually is it necessary to separate identical twins (who are not numerous) at the time of birth. And in the rare event of that being unavoidable, efforts are usually made to maintain some contact between the twins. Often, they are brought up within the same family. Another practical problem is that those rare and unhappy circumstances in which the separation of identical twins cannot be prevented are not ones in which it is probable that accurate records will be made. However, in order for a properly controlled research study to be undertaken it is essential for such records to be available.

Because of these difficulties, it has been far from easy to locate properly documented cases of identical twins who have been separated at birth. All the same, a number of studies of identical twins reared together and apart have been reported: evidence has been collected from around a hundred such individuals. Unfortunately, however, very few of the published reports actually describe research based on comparisons between twins reared together and ones who really were separated at birth. Far more commonly, the actual comparisons are between twins who have been reared entirely together and ones reared *partly* apart. In some studies the latter category contains pairs of twins who have spent as much as four years together. Typically these are the earliest years of the twins' lives, and therefore ones that are especially crucial.

Clearly, then, what appear to be studies of twins reared together and apart turn out to be something less than that. This is a serious defect. And the deficiencies of these investigations are compounded by the fact that the research reports tend to lack detailed information concerning important potential influences such as the precise times at which the twins were separated.

To identify these defects is not to criticize the researchers who have undertaken the investigations. The limitations have been virtually inevitable. Research has been impeded both by the rarity of situations in which identical twins have been separated at birth, and by the difficult underlying circumstances. Fortunately, in the future it will not be necessary to rely largely on twin studies for information concerning the long-term effects of variability in people's genetic materials. Direct mapping of genetic information ought to make it possible to obtain a more accurate account of genetic influences.

There have already been efforts to get round the problems mentioned above. However, that is not as easy at it might appear to be. For example, it seems sensible to ask whether genetically different individuals raised in similar home backgrounds are more or less alike than genetically similar people brought up in very different environments. Unfortunately, however, arriving at a simple answer to that question is ruled out by the fact that variability in one situation may depend largely upon genetic differences, but in a different set of circumstances be affected more powerfully by environmental differences.

A hypothetical illustration provided by Stephen Gould demonstrates how that can be possible. He considers the possible influences upon the heights of men living in a poor Indian village (Gould, 1984). Height is known to be highly heritable, and the height of the sons in the village is closely related to their fathers' height.

In one generation nutritional deficits are common among the villagers. In this generation the average height is around 5 feet 6 inches. The tallest individuals measure around 5 feet 8. However, by a few generations later there has been a marked change. By this time average height has risen to 5 feet 10 inches. Note that this has happened despite the fact that height is highly heritable. In effect then, in spite of the marked heritability of height, the changed circumstances of life have rapidly led to a situation in which the heights of even the tallest individuals from the first generation are exceeded by many individuals.

In summary, it is true that genetic variability can have consequences that affect high abilities. But as we have seen, these outcomes are not straightforwardly predictable. And the issue of whether or not there exist influences on people's capabilities that take the predictable form associated with the notion of a gift or talent still remains an open question.

Innate gifts and talents revisited: the evidence

Are innate gifts and talents real or fictitious? I mentioned, in Chapter 1, some findings that have been assumed to provide conclusive evidence of the existence of talents. For example, there have been reports of certain exceptional skills for which there appeared to be no alternative explanation. However, on closer examination it has become evident that the skills can quite readily be explained in other ways. What other evidence exists for or against the view that innate gifts and talents are real rather than being mythical?

In attempting to answer this question, my colleagues and I (Howe *et al.*, 1998) have looked at three kinds of evidence.

First, we have examined findings that appear to support the innate talent account, according to which a minority of people possess innate qualities that help to make it possible for a particular individual to excel at a specific area of expertise.

Second, we have looked at evidence that appears to contradict or disprove the talent account.

Third, we have examined the possibility that there may be alternative reasons for those differences between people in their capabilities that have been assumed to provide justification for belief in the innate talent account. In other words, we have asked what it might be, if it is not innate gifts and talents, that makes people differ in their capabilities.

Evidence appearing to support the talent account

Various findings have been put forward in the belief that they form evidence to support the innate talent account. For example, there are plenty of reports of very young children who learn to talk early, often in the first year, and gain various other abilities, such as musical skills or competence at a foreign language, much earlier than usual, apparently in the absence of special learning opportunities.

As evidence, however, these reports have the limitation of being anecdotal. They are typically descriptions made by a parent, who is often describing events that took place some time ago. Very few of the cases have been objectively assessed or verified at the time by a trained researcher. When researchers have been able to examine the circumstances, it usually emerges that accompanying any unusual feats or achievement by the child there have been unusual learning experiences, or special training opportunities (see, for example, Fowler, 1983; Feldman, 1986). The prodigious childhood accomplishments of Mozart are often mentioned in this context. It is certainly true that his early skills were exceptional, but it is equally true that the opportunities which his father provided for his son to learn about music were quite extraordinary (Howe, 1997).

Another kind of evidence that has been regarded as supporting the talent account takes the form of the verified existence of a musical skill, the capacity to identify 'perfect' or absolute pitch. This usually appears early in life or not at all, and is only present in a minority of children. On the surface at least, it appears to provide a clear embodiment of innate musical talent.

However, although usually acquired early, it appears that perfect pitch is nevertheless a learned capacity, the reason why is not often acquired unless it is gained early being that it is much easier to learn before a child has established a firm habit of listening to meaningful groups of musical sounds rather than attending to single notes. It can, although with difficulty, be acquired later in life. Moreover, the case for perceiving perfect pitch as an instance of an innate talent is weakened by the fact that, although it conveys some advantages on young musicians, perfect pitch is not essential, and it is not possessed by many outstanding musicians.

Providing a third kind of evidence that is consistent with the talent account are numerous reports of studies in which correlations have been observed between high abilities and physical assessments of brain functioning. Essentially, there are clear differences between individuals in various brain activities, and these differences are related to differences in capabilities.

But this evidence does not necessarily support the talent account. One problem with it is that there are almost no measures of brain activities that are selectively associated with particular specific abilities. Another problem is a logical one. Understandably, it is generally assumed that if a difference between people in the physical operation in their brains is associated with differences in their capability, that finding forms evidence that the physical or biological difference is the cause of the differences in abilities.

However, in some cases closer investigation has shown that such an inference concerning cause and effect is unjustified. One broad reason for that conclusion is that the fact that two qualities are related is rarely sufficient evidence for the existence of such a cause and effect association (Howe, 1988c). A more specific reason for questioning it is that in certain studies it has been observed that a difference in the biological functioning of the brain is likely to have been at least partly the *consequence* of learning and experience, and certainly not its cause. For example, in violinists it is found that the part of the brain representing the fingers of the left hand (which undertake the fingering of the strings of the instrument) is larger than in other people. Moreover, the younger a person started playing the violin, the bigger the difference (Schlaug *et al.*, 1995). These findings strongly suggest that the brain differences between violinists and others are the consequence of early musical experiences, rather than an initial cause of expertise.

Evidence appearing to refute the talent account

I mentioned, in Chapter 1, a number of instances, such as the early sitting activities of the African infants observed by Charles Super, in which special abilities that appeared to be totally inexplicable, except by assuming that innate talents were involved, proved on closer examination to be easy to explain. In all cases it turned out that the individuals involved had been exposed to special experiences or learning opportunities, although these did not necessarily involve any formal teaching or training. Chapter 1 also described some training studies in which people who watched individuals performing certain unusual skills were convinced that the performers must have possessed special talents. In reality, however, the performers were ordinary people who had been selected more or less at random to receive special training.

There have been a number of other studies in which researchers have looked for, but failed to find, the kinds of early differences that could only be explained by assuming that innate talents were a contributing influence. For example, in studies of unusually competent young musicians that were undertaken by myself and my colleagues, there was a marked lack of very early signs of special potential, except for ones that were specifically encouraged by parents (Howe *et al.*, 1995). Similarly, in a study of outstanding young American concert pianists, very early signs of special ability were strikingly absent, and even by the time that these instrumentalists had been receiving intensive training for six or seven years, only in a minority of cases could their eventual outstanding success have been predicted

(Sosniak, 1985; 1990). A similar lack of inexplicable very early signs of special potential was observed among experts in a variety of areas of expertise, including art, mathematics, tennis, and swimming (Bloom, 1985).

Further evidence of an absence of the kinds of underlying differences that would be indicative of the role of innate talents has been obtained in studies examining young people's rate of progress. Contrary to the view that there are some individuals who can progress much faster than others, and with considerably less effort, the evidence suggest that all learners have to devote considerable amounts of time to practising. Sloboda *et al.*, (1996) found that in order to progress from one musical grade to another, the most able of the young children being studied had to spend just as much time practising as the less able did.

Conclusion: alternative causes of the phenomena attributed to innate talents

Why is it that people differ so much in the extent to which they seem capable of various kinds of expertise? If innate gifts and talents are not the cause, what is? In fact, there is absolutely no reason to believe that there is one single cause of human variability. There are numerous causes. As a consequence of their differing experiences and their differing genes people live sharply varying lives, and their minds become furnished in contrasting ways.

The idea that there exist innate gifts or talents is essentially a theory. It asserts that there exist identifiable innate differences between people in their potentials for excelling at various areas of competence. As with any theory, the truth or falsity of the talent account needs to be verified, and such verification is achieved largely by looking at the evidence. Most of the evidence that appears to favour the talent account takes the form of early manifestations of special abilities, the acquisition of which does not appear to be explicable in other ways.

But as we have seen, there are problems with this evidence. Some of it is anecdotal, depending on the unreliable memories of parents. In a number of cases more systematic studies have failed to confirm the truth of the anecdotal accounts. In cases where the early appearance of special skills has been verified, it has been observed there have been special factors that could account for those skills, in the form of unusual experiences or opportunities.

In short, there are strong grounds for saying that there are few if any items of evidence that only the innate talent account can explain. That does not mean that the existence of innate talents has been positively disproved, and it is also true some researchers have arrived at conclusions that are different from the ones reached here (see, for example, Winner, 1996). However, if a theory relates to a postulated cause of events, but it is found that those events can be entirely satisfactorily explained in other ways, as a consequence of observable causes such as practising and exposure to learning experiences, rather than unobservable ones such as innate talents, the theory is bound to appear somewhat suspect. In my opinion, although belief in gifts and innate talents is widespread, there has never been any entirely convincing evidence to justify that belief. The various ways in which children's lives differ – their differing opportunities to form preferences and tastes, the differing ways in which they spend their time, their differing attitudes to learning experiences, their differing habits and willingness to spend time practising, the differing events that gain and sustain their attention – combine to make it inevitable that there will be considerable variability in the extent to which young people equip themselves for acquiring particular kinds of capabilities. So apart from its other defects, the innate talent account suffers from being a redundant theory, because it purports to explain phenomena that have already been adequately explained.

Chapter 8

Helping young people to learn

The belief lingers on that exceptional abilities are only gained by individuals who are born possessing exceptional talents or inherited gifts. As we have seen, that belief is certainly false, even though it is true that genetic variability is among the factors that can influence human accomplishments. Despite the possibility that genetic influences may convey advantages or disadvantages, there is solid evidence that most young children, if given enough opportunities and sufficient encouragement, are able to learn considerably more than children normally do. The majority of young people are quite capable of reaching high levels of competence in any of a large variety of areas of achievement.

Although our knowledge about the circumstances in which a few individuals gain outstanding abilities is far from being complete, we do know enough to be certain that it is within our power to increase the numbers of young people who become capable of mastering difficult human accomplishments. There will never be any simple formula for manufacturing genius, but, as we have seen, there is plenty of evidence that impressive capabilities can be gained by the majority of ordinary people, provided that opportunities for learning are made available, as well as sufficient support and encouragement, and enough time for training and practice.

In reality, unfortunately, many of today's children do not have access to the opportunities and the other forms of support that kindle high abilities. Consequently, these children never achieve the goals they might otherwise have reached. Of course, even if rich opportunities for learning were more widely available, not every child would take full advantage of them. But as we saw in Chapter 2, those young people whose parents can ensure that their early lives are lived in circumstances rich in interest and stimulation, with plenty of encouragement to gain the kinds of skills and knowledge that allow a person to make good sense of the world, are far more likely to grow up into unusually capable young adults than are children who do not have such opportunities.

Impediments to parental encouragement

So why are we not doing more to increase the proportion of young people who are capable of mastering exceptional skills? Why are there so few policy decisions aimed at achieving this? What is holding people back?

One inhibiting factor is the widely shared view that radical educational improvements can only be achieved via schools and school-based educational systems. Consequently, the possibility that educational policy changes that are not firmly based in the schools might be enormously influential is often ignored, and rarely given serious attention. That is unfortunate because, as finding after finding has repeatedly shown, many of the most potent influences that affect the likelihood of a child developing into an exceptionally able young person are ones that are exerted within the child's own home, and stem from the actions of individuals in the child's own family.

Another inhibiting influence is the ignorance of many parents concerning the extent to which their children's progress depends upon their own actions and attitudes as parents. In fact, as we discovered in Chapter 3, the acquisition of even the most fundamental and far-reaching human skills, including language, is accelerated when ordinary parents take simple steps to intensify the help and encouragement they provide.

Obviously, parents who do not realize how much they can do to aid their children's progress will be unlikely to make special efforts to accelerate early development. A parent needs to have some confidence that a major investment of energy and patience will have some positive effects. Many adults are unaware of the real improvement that even a relatively small effort on a parent's part may bring about. If it was more widely known that relatively modest interventions designed to accelerate the development of language skills can lead to substantial gains, or if more adults appreciated the fact that it is worth making efforts to stimulate a child's comprehension well before the child actually begins to speak, many parents might show increased interest in their children's early education.

Yet another factor is that many of those parents who are aware, however dimly, that their own parental practices can have far-reaching consequences, so far as their children's progress is concerned, are only too conscious of their own limitations as teachers. They feel that they do not know what to do, or how, in order to give effective help and encouragement.

The problem identified here is a real one, and addressing it ought to be a prime focus of educational policies aimed at helping young children to learn. Undoubtedly, some parents are better equipped to help than others, by virtue of temperament, attitude, and their own knowledge, and the degree of literacy they have arrived at, and more adequately prepared to act as guides for their children. But it is not only those parents who are inarticulate or poorly educated who experience problems caused by lack of know-how and expertise in teaching young children. In one of the studies described in Chapter 3, which investigated the effects of giving parents simple advice about techniques to employ when reading to young children, it was found that the children of those parents who had received simple instructions made considerably more progress at language skills than another group of children. This was despite the fact that the other children had conscientious parents who all read to their children, and spent just as much time doing so as did the parents in the specially instructed group. Findings such as this demonstrate that even those children whose parents are relatively expert as guides for their children, and highly committed to helping children to learn, stand to gain a great deal from policies designed to help adults to guide children more effectively.

Parents tend to overestimate the degree of technical expertise in teaching that is required in order to give a child assistance with learning. Generally speaking, the most important qualities required are sensitivity, patience, enthusiasm, common sense, and perseverance, rather than particular instructional skills or teaching techniques. Parents are especially effective as guides and teachers when they spend time patiently explaining things, drawing their child's attention to important objects and events, answering children's questions, posing questions that encourage children to concentrate and reflect, and doing all they can to make the child's world more understandable.

Yet even if it is true that many parents underestimate their own competence as teachers of their children, the sheer fact that they *feel* themselves to be incapable indicates that they need guidance, and at present that is in short supply, particularly where it is most needed. For many parents, particularly those who are not highly educated, vestiges of a 'leave it to the school' and 'teacher knows best' attitude remain too influential.

A final reason for reluctance about implementing activities that would accelerate children's progress is that many people are understandably anxious that efforts to extend and intensify learning in young children can have adverse outcomes as well as positive ones. As was indicated in Chapter 4, some of the fears and anxieties are by no means unjustified. It is all too easy for parents who, for whatever reasons, are particularly strongly bent on maximizing a child's accomplishments, to act in ways that create difficulties for the child. In some cases the child suffers from the pressure of parental expectations, in others the child is deprived of opportunities for play, or other social experiences that contribute to normal development.

In yet other instances too much specialization or an insufficiency of opportunities to make one's own choices, may result in the child failing to gain abilities that are needed in order to become able to function as a fully independent adult, make mature personal decisions, and gain an inner-directed sense of purpose. Those parents who are unusually committed to their childrens's success are sometimes prone to become dependent on the vicarious success that is provided by a child's achievements. Such parents may be rather insensitive to children's needs that are unrelated to the particular kinds of accomplishments that the parent values most, or unaware of personal difficulties that the child is experiencing.

The parent who sets out with the firm intention of making a child into an outstanding musician, scientist, sportsperson, mathematician, or whatever, may be sending the child into a dangerous minefield. But a parent who has the more realistic goal of giving a child the advantages of having an unusually good start in life, and is prepared to let the child make decisions about how to make use of those advantages, is far more likely to see the child develop into a capable and independent adult (Howe, 1988e; 1988f; 1989c; 1990a; 1990b). So far as the early lives of most children are concerned, there is considerable leeway for parents to increase their efforts to assist and encourage children to learn basic skills, without invoking any danger of a child being harmed either by too much pressure or by the kind of extreme specialization that could lead to diminished opportunities for some of the experiences of a normal childhood. The fact that a highly intensive 'hot house' kind of early childhood regime may have undesirable effects ought not to dissuade parents from making reasonable efforts to help a child to progress further and faster than is usual.

For some parents one more reason for doing little or nothing to encourage high achievements is simply that not every adult places much value on such achievements. Not every parent attaches high importance to, say, the ability to perform instrumental music. Similarly, parents differ in the value they attach to the goal of helping their children to gain abilities that are intellectual in nature. Some parents would argue that modern civilization already places too much pressure on children to succeed and excel, and would resist the very idea of helping young children to extend their abilities.

Practicalities of helping young children to learn: some parents' approaches

Precisely how do you help infants and young children to learn? It is worth emphasizing that the majority of those parents who are unusually successful at helping their children to learn do not depend on any special or unusual instructional techniques. And, as we saw in Chapter 4, the likelihood of a child gaining abilities considerably younger than usual does not seem to be greatly affected by whether the help given by the parents takes the form of structured instruction of a relatively formal kind or is largely informal and unstructured. That seems to have made little or no difference in the past, in the case of nineteenth-century child prodigies, nor does it seem to be an important source of variability in the achievements of children today.

Reports on their children's upbringing written by the parents of child prodigies, and autobiographical accounts by prodigies themselves, have been fertile sources of information, some of it quite detailed, about the varied ways in which people have tried to assist their children's progress during the years of early childhood. Despite the marked variability in the different parents' approaches (as seen, for example, in the large differences in the degree to which their didactic plans have taken a formal structure), many of the parents whose efforts have been particularly successful have shared a number of qualities. Almost always, these parents have been willing to give large amounts of time and attention to the early education of their children. In some instances, even with parents whose methods of instruction have been highly informal, there has been – eventually, if not at first – a degree of systematic planning in their approach.

In many cases the parents have been convinced that their child was inherently ordinary, and they have sometimes held firm views concerning the desirability of early intellectual training that sharply contrasted with prevailing opinions. A number of the parents have drawn attention to the extent to which opportunities to learn are wasted in most people's childhoods, and some have been highly critical of the wastefulness of school-based educational systems. Some of these parents have held very strong views concerning individuals' duties towards other people: they have tended to believe that the gaining of high intellectual achievements, and the proper exploitation of them, are as much obligations as rewards.

These parents' educational methods and techniques of instruction were nothing like so untypical of their times as were their broader attitudes towards education in early childhood and their awareness of the potential strength of its effects. It seems that most of these parents, quirky, arrogant, and insensitive as some of them were, had the good sense to be distrustful of the notion that it is possible to make easy short-cuts in the education of a human child. Their awareness that learning needs to be interesting and enjoyable did not make them insensitive to the fact that the process of becoming extraordinarily able demands considerable effort and patience on the part of learner and teacher alike, and is inevitably time-consuming, and sometimes arduous as well.

For example, the elder Karl Witte, writing about his son Karl's upbringing at the beginning of the nineteenth century, was sure of his priorities. His first intention had been to ensure that the younger Karl would he healthy, strong, active, and happy. The father reported with justified pride, 'and in this, as everybody knows, I have succeeded' (Witte, 1975, p. 53). He was also determined from the outset that his son should become outstandingly able. In the face of a climate of opinion in which it was almost universally agreed that a person's achievements largely depended upon inborn 'aptitudes', he was convinced that these were considerably less important than a child's education in the first five or six years.

The elder Witte's description of some of the ways in which his infant son was encouraged to learn reads almost as if it came from an account of the methods adopted by modern researchers such as Fowler and his co-workers to promote language development a century and a half later. The father records that his son,

> learned many things in the arms of his mother and in my own, such as one rarely thinks of imparting to children. He learned to know and name all the objects in ten different rooms, the rooms themselves, the staircase, the yard, the garden, the stable, the well, the barn, – everything from the greatest to the smallest, was frequently shown and clearly and plainly named to him, and he was encouraged to name the objects as plainly as possible. Whenever he spoke correctly he was fondled and praised. When, however, he failed, we said in a decidedly cooler manner, 'Mother (or Father), Karl cannot yet pronounce this or that word!'... Consequently he took great pains to know and correctly name all objects. (Witte, 1975, p. 71)

Language was seen by the prescient elder Witte as the key to intellectual competence. Acquiring the mother tongue, he said, 'makes the child intelligent at an early time, for it puts his attention and his several mental powers continuously in action. He is obliged always to search, distinguish, compare, prefer, report, choose, in short he must work, that is, think' (Witte, 1975, p. 75).

The child's parents took great pains to expose him to as varied a range of experiences as they could provide: these ranged from the familiar to the exotic. Consequently, while he was still a young child, Karl encountered not only watermills and windmills, and owls and bats, but also concerts, dramas, and operas, and lions and ostriches and elephants. And the parents took care to draw Karl's attention to important aspects of the objects they showed him. They also explained to Karl all the things he came across, and discussed them in his presence, so that he understood the objects he perceived not 'by merely staring at them, as children generally know them, but thoroughly' (Witte, 1975, p. 81). In this and other ways the parents provided countless instances of the kind of mediated learning which, as we saw in Chapter 2, Reuven Feuerstein regards as crucial for today's infants and children. Karl Witte's parents were careful to talk to him about all the events they showed him, and they made sure that he noticed whatever was important. They regularly asked him whether he liked what he was seeing, so that the child 'became accustomed to what he had seen and heard, and he himself addressed us, enquired, reported, retorted, and so on' (Witte, 1975, p. 81).

Like Feuerstein, but many years earlier, Witte recognized that valuable abilities, such as that of being able to discriminate between different objects, are most likely to be acquired when an adult can provide learning experiences that are designed to direct the child's attention in ways that promote learning. And like all good teachers, the father knew the value of play and games. He was convinced that it was never too early for parents to engage their infants in playful activities. He stated that, with enough imagination, nearly all common objects could be turned into toys, a course of action that he regarded as much more effective than the practice of buying expensive toys but failing to give the child proper guidance in the use of them. But building blocks did meet his approval.

When Witte judged that his son was ready to learn to read, the father was sufficiently astute to appreciate the importance of motivation, so he went to some lengths to make sure that his child would want to read. When Karl was aged three, his father bought ten sets of German letters, the largest being three inches high, which were pasted on pictures of wood. He invented a family game in which the letters were all thrown into a box. Mother, father and child would sit together on the carpet, where they carefully mixed up the letters in the box, and then picked out one letter at a time. Each letter 'was carefully and solemnly surveyed and loudly and distinctly named. It went from hand to hand, and everybody did the same' (Witte, 1975, p. 224).

After a few quarter-hour sessions of the game each day for several days, Karl had learned all the letters, quickly and painlessly. The father then began to help his son learn to read syllables and words. At one stage Witte found that the child had been temporarily put off learning to read because his mother had been teaching him in a manner that was too formal and heavy-handed. After that, the father was even more careful to delay teaching new reading skills until Karl had shown a desire to learn them. Only after the child had made repeated requests did he start helping him learn to write, and even then he avoided formal teaching.

Even today, we can learn much from the elder Karl Witte's bold experiment. This fiercely independent man, who had the courage to trust his own judgement in the face of insults and ridicule, and persist with a course of action that many people told him could only fail, brought to the task of educating his son qualities of imagination, persistence, patience, and above all, an ability, uncommon now and much rarer in his time, of being able to understand a young child's point of view. In particular, Witte realized how enormously important it is for a child to want to learn, and he was therefore careful to make his son's learning experiences informal and playful, and to delay introducing new skills until the son's eagerness to acquire them was already apparent.

There is more than one way to educate a young child. The way in which James Mill approached the upbringing of his son John Stuart Mill, described in the son's famous *Autobiography* (Mill, 1971), first published five months after his death in 1873, was much more formal and more tightly structured than Witte's. John Stuart Mill's early education contained larger elements of severity and compulsion than the younger Witte's seems to have done. This might account, at least in part, for the fact that while the mature John Stuart was second to none intellectually, he nevertheless suffered periods of serious depression.

John Stuart Mill set out to provide as full an account of his unusual childhood as he could give, because, he said,

> in an age in which education, and its improvement, are the subject of more, if not of profounder study than at any former period of English history, it may be useful that there should be some record of an education that was unusual and remarkable, and which, whatever else it may have done, has proved how much more than is commonly supposed may be taught, and well taught, in those early years which, in the common modes of what is called instruction, are little better than wasted. (Mill, 1971, p. 5)

Mill begins his *Autobiography* by emphasizing just how hard his father had to labour in order to educate his children at home at the same time as working on his lengthy *History of India*. At least in the case of John Stuart, who was the oldest child, James Mill exerted 'an amount of labour, care, and perseverance rarely, if ever, employed for a similar purpose, in endeavouring to give, according to his own conception, the highest order of intellectual education' (Mill, 1971, p. 7).

We learn nothing of Mill's early language development, for the obvious reason that no-one remembers this stage of their own life, or of his first steps towards reading. The first records of his education that appear in the *Autobiography* are not taken from memory but are reproduced from what others told Mill later in his life. For instance, Mill informs us that he has no memory of the time when he began to learn Greek, but adds that he has been informed that it was when he was three years old. His earliest recollection about learning Greek is of memorizing lists of words, paired with the English equivalents, written out on cards by his father. Greek grammar was taught him some years later. He reports that he began Latin in his eighth year, and lists a number of Greek and Latin authors that he was required to translate at around that time. He adds that until he had learned Latin, and became able to make use of a Greek and Latin lexicon, he was forced to ask his father about the meaning of every word encountered in his lessons which he did not already know. For several years this resulted in the father having to submit to incessant interruptions, despite which, the son notes admiringly, James Mill continued to make steady progress on his own monumental *History of India*.

Formal instruction in John Stuart Mill's early childhood seems to have been restricted to Greek and arithmetic. He disliked the latter intensely. But equally importantly, the child was strongly encouraged to read, and he spent a large part of each day doing so, mainly from books of history, although his reading was wide and varied. Before breakfast, he would accompany his father on walks in the country, and during the walks the son would give an account of what he had read on the previous day, jogging his memory with notes that he had made on slips of paper while he had been reading. He reports that this exercise was a voluntary rather than a prescribed one, but it is safe to assume that the idea of doing it came from the father rather than from the son. Most of the books that John Stuart Mill read at this time (they would probably have been chosen for him from his father's library) were ones that contained narrative passages which an unusually knowledgeable and intelligent child would be able to understand, and even enjoy, without too much difficulty. For example, Mill writes with enthusiasm of a book entitled *Philip the Second and Third* by a Robert Watson, in which 'The heroic defence of the knights of Malta against the Turks, and of the revolted provinces of the Netherlands against Spain, excited in me an intense and lasting interest.' He adds that his father was fond of putting into his hands books which 'exhibited men of energy and resource in unusual circumstances, struggling against difficulties and overcoming them', as well as books of discovery, such as descriptions of the voyages of Drake, Cook, and Anson, which any boy would have found exciting. But he was given very few children's books, and he notes that his father only permitted them 'very sparingly', although the boy was allowed to read *Robinson Crusoe*, which was a source of delight throughout his childhood.

As a child, John Stuart Mill both admired and feared his father, and in the *Autobiography* he tries hard to give a balanced view of the father's qualities as a teacher. Sometimes James Mill seems to have acted with unreasonable severity. For instance, John Stuart was forced to practise writing verses, which he found a most disagreeable task. When, inspired by Pope's translation of Homer's Iliad, he spontaneously attempted, although (he says) without much success, to do something of the same kind himself, he found that the activity, which might have been expected to cease at that point, 'was continued by command' (Mill, 1971, p. 19).

James Mill did at least take care to explain to his son why he was compelling him to do this and other hated tasks. On occasions he could be a highly sensitive parent, and he often encouraged his son to express himself without fear of criticism. Writing of a childish attempt to produce a history of Rome, John Stuart Mill records that, to his relief, his father had the tact to avoid asking to see what had been written, so that the son did not experience the unpleasant situation of being under the father's critical eye.

Whatever its faults, it cannot he denied that the upbringing and education that James Mill provided for his son gave the latter a superb intellectual grounding. The fact that John Stuart Mill became one of the great thinkers of his age was due in no small part to his father's pedagogical efforts. James Mill's strengths as an educator were in many respects different from the elder Witte's, but in common to both fathers' approaches, apart from their admirable diligence and conscientiousness as teachers, was the enormous emphasis they placed on the necessity of the student having a clear understanding of what was to be learned, and becoming able to think for himself. Both stressed the importance of meaningfulness and comprehensibility, and each was severely critical of current educational practices that involved rote learning and drills, and the meaningless repetition of information. A passage in which John

Stuart Mill draws attention to his father's insistence on the importance of understanding as well as his avoidance of drill methods can serve as a summary of what was best in the education which James Mill provided for his son.

> There was one cardinal point in this training... which, more than anything else, was the cause of whatever good it effected. Most boys or youths have had much knowledge drilled into them, have their mental capacities not strengthened, but over-laid by it. They are crammed with mere facts, and with the opinions or phrases of other people, and these are accepted as a substitute for the power to form opinions of their own... Mine, however, was not an education of cram. My father never permitted anything which I learnt, to degenerate into a mere exercise of memory. He strove to make the understanding not only go along with every step of the teaching, but if possible, precede it. (Mill, 1971, p. 35)

Mill's education was also unusual for its time in not containing a large element of religion. The parents of other child prodigies who were broadly contemporary with John Stuart Mill saw religious knowledge as both a means of providing education and a reason for gaining it. With John Ruskin, the great art critic, who was born in 1819, the Bible provided the focus of most of the early instruction which his devoutly evangelical mother provided for him. The following extract from a letter she wrote to her husband when John was still only two years old gives an idea of the serious and the predominantly religious tone of the child's early upbringing.

> We get on very well with our reading he knows all the commandments but the second perfectly and the Lords prayer – his memory astonishes me and his understanding too. (Burd, 1973, p. 109)

In fact, the young Ruskin had to read aloud from the Bible – two or three chapters a day, seven days per week – throughout his entire childhood. So intense a preoccupation with religious matters would be unusual in parents today, but in other respects the childhoods of those twentieth-century child prodigies whose early education has been recorded in reasonable detail seem not to have been very different, on the whole, from those of the earlier generations. As we have seen, behind the accelerated early progress of exceptionally precocious children there have often been parents who have been unusually active as educators, and unusually serious-minded and conscientious in their efforts to help their children acquire important intellectual skills while they were still very young.

As we would expect, the twentieth-century parents transmit to their children their own interests and values and preoccupations. For example, it is not uncommon to find modern parents encouraging a child to gain expertise in mathematics or the sciences. That kind of emphasis is a surprisingly recent phenomenon: Darwin's father, although enthusiastic about science, never encouraged his son to think of biology as a vocation, probably because prior to Victoria's reign there was scant possibility of an Englishman making any kind of living as a research scientist. By the time Norbert Wiener was a boy at the beginning of the twentieth century, things had changed dramatically, and opportunities for scientists and mathematicians to gain paid employment were becoming relatively numerous. Science books played a part in Wiener's education from a very early stage. On his fourth birthday his father gave him a volume on natural history, and soon afterwards Norbert read a children's book on elementary science which included discussions of such non-childish topics as the nature of light. By seven he had read a number of books on chemistry, physiology, botany, zoology, and various branches of physics, and was conducting chemical experiments under the supervision of an instructor whom his father had hired to teach him chemistry (Wiener, 1953).

The changes that have occurred over the generations in the broad approaches taken by parents towards the early education of their offspring have been considerably fewer and smaller than the changes in the particular topics they have encouraged their children to learn. Nowadays it is probably more common than in the past for parents to employ games and play sessions in order to arouse a child's interest in a new skill, just as the elder Karl Witte did at the beginning of the nineteenth century, than to adopt the more coercive approach of a parent such as James Mill. But there is no direct link of cause and effect between parental teaching style and a child's successes. Although it is tempting to assume that the relative severity of the early education received by John Stuart Mill and John Ruskin was the cause of their neuroticism, we would be wise to remember that the education received in early childhood by William Sidis, who was more neurotic than either of them, was not at all severe. That the playful tradition of the elder Witte is still alive in today's parents is demonstrated by numerous remarks collected in the course of the Chicago-based interview studies of exceptional young adults that were described in Chapters 2 and 4. There are many examples of a child's interest being caught through games. A young mathematician recalls, for instance,

> When we were very young, both my brother and I liked to play games. My father was especially good at playing games with us and keeping it fun. I remember him telling me some really exciting things, which would turn out to be some kind of math, and I would play with the ideas. My father was a sensitive teacher, and I'm sure he did all kinds of subtle things that didn't seem like teaching. (Gustin, 1985, p. 281)

Conclusion: chance and fortune in human life

To end on a different note, we would be prudent to acknowledge that our best efforts to explain, understand, and predict the course of individual human lives are pre-empted at many points by chance influences that we can neither foresee nor control. As we discovered in Chapter 5, even the likelihood that someone will be regarded as a genius depends as much on other people's largely unpredictable reactions to the individual's contributions as it does on that person's actual achievements. Chance factors can produce sudden changes which confound scientific predictions. An injury, a plane accident, or even a sudden infatuation may alter an individual's progress in ways that no-one could predict.

The significance of particular lifetime events may not be apparent until long after they taken place. When the writer

H. G. Wells was seven years old he broke his leg. That is hardly the kind of happening that one would wish on a boy of that age. But the effect of that accident in his particular case was to encourage an already bookish young child, confined by his injury to spending long hours in bed, to devote even more of his time to reading. His injury almost certainly contributed to the fact that Wells became an unusually knowledgeable young person, and in later years a major author and an intellectual force to be reckoned with. Another eminent writer, Charles Dickens, reported that in his childhood, too, being confined to bed (because of illness) had a strong influence on his development as a reader. Dickens commented that sickness brought the great advantage of encouraging him to read. And for some of today's children as well, having to spend weeks or months in bed can be the spark that kindles an intense interest. David Feldman (1986) mentions the case of a brilliant young chess player who first began to take the game seriously when at the age of five his normally energetic physical activities were suddenly curtailed by a broken collarbone.

But in all likelihood, for every child who has profited from injury or illness there have been others for whom the only consequences have been negative ones. Human individuality dictates that whatever we discover about the effects that a particular event have had on one individual may tell us little or nothing about the likely effects of a similar event upon someone else. As Howard Gruber has noted, each person incorporates or is otherwise affected by the happenings of his or her lifetime in a distinctive and unique way.

We cannot map people's lives in advance, but much can be done to make desirable outcomes more likely. Acquiring high abilities is one such outcome. We can and should act to make it happen more often.

References

Ainsworth, M. D. S., Bell, S. M. and Stayton, D. J. (1974) Infant–mother attachment and social development: socialisation as a product of reciprocal responsiveness to signals. In Richards, M. P. M. (ed.), *The Integration of a Child into a Social World*. London: Cambridge University Press.

Bamberger, J. (1986) Cognitive issues in the development of musically gifted children. In Sternberg, R. J. and Davidson, J. E. (eds), *Conceptions of Giftedness*. Cambridge: Cambridge University Press.

Berry, C. (1981) The Nobel scientists and the origins of scientific achievement. *British Journal of Sociology*, **32**: 381–91.

Berry, C. (1990) On the origins of exceptional intellectual and cultural achievement. In Howe, M. J. A. (ed.), *Encouraging the Development of Exceptional Abilities and Talents*. Leicester: The British Psychological Society.

Biederman, L. and Shiffrar, M. M. (1987) Sexing day-old chicks: a case study and expert systems analysis of a difficult perceptual-learning task. *Journal of Experimental Psychology: Learning, Memory and Cognition*, **13**: 640–5.

Bloom, B. S. (ed.) (1985) *Developing Talent in Young People*. New York: Ballantine.

Blum, D. (1989) A process larger than oneself. *The New Yorker*, May 1, 41–74.

Bradley, L. and Bryant, P. E. (1983) Categorizing sounds and learning to read in preschoolers. *Journal of Educational Psychology*, **68**: 680–8.

Brady, P. T. (1970) The genesis of absolute pitch. *Journal of the Acoustical Society of America*, **48**: 883–7.

Bryant, P. E. and Bradley, L. (1985) *Children's Reading Problems: Psychology and Education*. Oxford: Blackwell.

Burd, V. A. (1973) *The Ruskin Family Letters: the Correspondence of John James Ruskin, His Wife, and Their Son, John, 1801–1843*, Vol. 1. London: Cornell University Press.

Bynner, J. M. and Romney, D. M. (1986) Intelligence, fact or artefact: alternative structures for cognitive abilities. *British Journal of Educational Psychology*, **56**: 13–23.

Ceci, S. J. (1990) *On Intelligence... More or Less: a Bio-ecological Theory of Intellectual Development*. Englewood Cliffs, New Jersey: Prentice-Hall.

Ceci, S. J., Baker, J. G. and Bronfenbrenner, U. (1987) The acquisition of simple and complex algorithms as a function of context. Unpublished manuscript. Ithaca, New York: Cornell University.

Charness, N., Krampe, R. and Mayr, U. (1996) The role of practice and coaching in entrepreneurial skill domains: an international comparison of life-span chess acquisition. In Ericsson, K. A. (ed.), *The Road to Excellence; The Acquisiton of Expert Performance in the Arts and Sciences, Sports and Games*. Mahwah, New Jersey: Erlbaum.

Chase, W. G. and Ericsson, K. A. (1981) Skilled memory. In Anderson, J. R. (ed.), *Cognitive Skills and their Acquisition*. Hillsdale, New Jersey: Erlbaum.

Clark, E. F. (1983) *George Parker Bidder: The Calculating Boy*. Bedford: KSL Publications.

Clark, R. W. (1979) *Einstein: the Life and Times*. London: Hodder & Stoughton.

Clarke-Stewart, K. A. (1973) Interactions between mothers and their young children: characteristics and consequences. *Monographs of the Society for Research in Child Development*, **38**, Serial No. 153.

Coles, G. (1987) *The Learning Mystique*. New York: Fawcett Ballantine.

Csikszentmihalyi, M. and Csikszentmihalyi, I. S. (1993) Family influences on the development of giftedness. In Bock, G. R. and Ackrill, K. (eds), *CIBA Foundation Symposium No 178: The Origins and Development of High Ability*. Chichester: Wiley.

Costall, A. (1985) The relativity of absolute pitch. In Howell, P., Cross, I. and West, R. (eds), *Musical Structure and Cognition*. London: Academic Press.

Davidson, H. P. (1931) An experimental study of bright, average and dull children at the four-year mental level. *Genetic Psychology Monographs*, **9**: 119–289.

Davidson, L. and Scripp, L. (1988) Young children's musical representations: windows on music cognition. In Sloboda, J. A. (ed.), *Generative Processes in Music: the Psychology of Performance, Improvisation, and Composition*. Oxford: Clarendon Press.

Dennis, W. (1941) Infant development under conditions of restricted practice and minimum social stimulation. *Genetic Psychology Monographs*, **23**: 143–89.

Dennis, W. and Dennis, M. G. (1951) Development under controlled environmental conditions. In Dennis, W. (ed.), *Readings in Child Psychology*. New York: Prentice-Hall.

Dowling, W. J. (1988) Tonal structure and children's early learning of music. In Sloboda, J. A. (ed.), *Generative Processes in Music: the Psychology of Performance, Improvisation, and Composition*. Oxford: Clarendon Press.

Dunn, J. and Plomin, R. (1990) *Separate Lives: Why Siblings are so Different*. New York: Basic Books.

Durkin, D. (1966) *Children Who Read Early*. New York: Teachers College Press, Columbia University.

Elder, G. H. (1988) Wartime losses and social bonding: influence across 40 years in men's lives. *Psychiatry*, **51**: 177–98.

Elder, G. H., Hastings, T. and Pavalko, E. (1989) Adult pathways to career distinction and disappointment. Paper presented at the Biennial Meeting of the Life History Research Society, Montreal, Canada.

Ericsson, K. A. (1985) Memory skill. *Canadian Journal of Psychology*, **39**: 188–231.

Ericsson, K. A. (1996) The acquisition of expert performance: An introduction to some of the issues. In Ericsson, K. A. (ed.), *The Road to Excellence; The Acquisiton of Expert Performance in the Arts and Sciences, Sports and Games*. Mahwah, New Jersey: Erlbaum.

Ericsson, K. A. and Charness, N. (1994) Expert performance: its structure and acquisition. *American Psychologist*, **49**: 725–47.

Ericsson, K. A. and Crutcher, R. J. (1988) The nature of exceptional performance. In Baltes, P. B., Featherman, D. L. and Lerner, R. M. (eds), *Life-span Development and Behavior*, Vol. 10.

Ericsson, K. A. and Faivre, I. A. (1988) What's exceptional about exceptional abilities? In Obler, L. K. and Fein, D. (eds), *The Exceptional Brain: Neuro-Psychology of Talent and Special Abilities*. New York: Guilford Press.

Feldman, D. H. (1986) *Nature's Gambit: Child Prodigies and the Development of Human Potential*. New York: Basic Books.

Feuerstein, R. (1980) *Instrumental Enrichment: an Intervention Program for Cognitive Modifiability*. Baltimore: University Park Press.

Feuerstein, R., Hoffman, M. B., Jensen, M. R. and Rand, Y. (1985) Instrumental enrichment, an intervention program for structural cognitive modifiability: theory and practice. In Segal, J. W., Chipman, S. F. and Glaser, R. (eds), *Thinking and Learning Skills*. Vol. 1: *Relating Instruction to Research*. Hillsdale, New Jersey: Erlbaum.

Fowler, W. (1981) Case studies of cognitive precocity; the role of exogenous and endogenous stimulation in early mental development. *Journal of Applied Developmental Psychology*, **2**: 319–67.

Fowler, W. (1983) *Potentials of Childhood*. Vol. 1: *A Historical View of Early Experience*. Vol. 2: *Studies in Early Developmental Learning*. Lexington, Massachusetts: Heath.

Fowler, W. (1986) Early experiences of great men and women mathematicians. In Fowler, W. (ed.), *Early Experience and the Development of Competence: No. 32, New Directions for Child Development*. San Francisco: Jossey-Bass.

Fowler, W. (1990) Early stimulation and the development of verbal talents. In Howe, M. J. A. (ed.), *Encouraging the Development of Exceptional Abilities and Talents*. Leicester: The British Psychological Society.

Fowler, W., Ogston, K., Roberts, G., Steane, D. and Swenson, A. (1983) *Potentials of Childhood*, Vol. 2: *Studies in Early Developmental Learning*. Lexington, Massachusetts: Heath.

Fox, L. H. (1976) The values of gifted youth. In Keating, D. P. (ed.), *Intellectual Talent: Research and Development. Proceedings of the Sixth Annual Hyman Blumberg Symposium on Research in Early Childhood Education*. Baltimore: Johns Hopkins University Press.

Freeman, J. (1985) A pedagogy for the gifted. In Freeman, J. (ed.), *The Psychology of Gifted Children*. Chichester: Wiley.

Fullard, W. G. (1967) Operant training of aural music discriminations with preschool children. *Journal of Research in Music Education*, **15**: 201–9.

Gardner, H. (1984) *Frames of Mind*. London: Heinemann.

Gesell, A. and Thompson, H. (1929) Learning and growth in identical infant twins: an experimental study by the method of co-twin control. *Genetic Psychology Monographs*, **6**: 1–124.

Glaser, R. (1996) Changing the agency for learning: acquiring expert performance. In Ericsson, K. A. (ed.), *The Road to Excellence; The Acquisiton of Expert Performance in the Arts and Sciences, Sports and Games*. Mahwah, New Jersey: Erlbaum.

Goldstein, D. M. (1976) Cognitive-linguistic functioning and learning to read in preschoolers, *Journal of Educational Psychology*, **68**: 680–8.

Gottfried, A. W. (1984) *Home Environment and Early Cognitive Development*. New York: Academic Press.

Gould, S. J. (1984) *The Mismeasure of Man*. Harmondsworth: Penguin Books.

Guess, D. (1969) A functional analysis of receptive language and productive speech: acquisition of the plural phoneme. *Journal of Applied Behavior Analysis*, **1**: 297–306.

Guess, D. and Baer, D. M. (1973) An analysis of individual differences in generalization between receptive and productive language in retarded children. *Journal of Applied Behaviour Analysis*, **6**: 311–29.

Gustin, W. C. (1985) The development of exceptional research mathematicians. In Bloom, B. S. (ed.), *Developing Talent in Young People*. New York: Ballantine Books.

Hamilton, J. (1997) *Turner: A Life*. London: Hodder & Stoughton.

Hamilton, M. L. (1977) Social learning and the transition from babbling to words. *Journal of Genetic Psychology*, **130**: 211–70.

Hart, B. and Risley, T. R (1990) *In vivo* language intervention: unanticipated general effects. *Journal of Applied Behaviour Analysis*, **13**: 407–32.

Hart, B. and Risley, T. (1995) *Meaningful Differences in Everyday Parenting and Intellectual Development in Young Children*. Baltimore: Brookes.

Hayes, J. R. (1981) *The Complete Problem Solver*. Philadelphia: The Franklin Institute Press.

Horn, J. (1986) Intellectual ability concepts. In Sternberg R. J. (ed.), *Advances in the Psychology of Human Intelligence*, Vol. 3. Hillsdale, New Jersey: Erlbaum.

Howe, M. J. A. (1977) *Television and Children*. London: New University Education.

Howe, M. J. A. (1980) *The Psychology of Human Learning*. New York: Harper & Row.

Howe, M. J. A. (1982) Biographical evidence and the development of outstanding individuals. *American Psychologist*, **37**: 1071–81.

Howe, M. J. A. (1983) *Introduction to the Psychology of Memory*. New York: Harper & Row. Republished in 1987 by University Press of America.

Howe, M. J. A. (1984) *A Teachers' Guide to the Psychology of Learning*. Oxford: Blackwell.

Howe, M. J. A. (1987) Using cognitive psychology to help students learn. In Richardson, J. T. E., Eysenck, M. W. and Warren Piper, D. (eds), *Student Learning: Research in Education and Cognitive Psychology*, pp. 135–46. Milton Keynes: SRHE/The Open University Press.

Howe, M. J. A. (1988a) Memory in mentally retarded 'idiots savants'. In Gruneberg, M. M., Morris, P. and Sykes, R. N. (eds), *Practical Aspects of Memory: Current Research and Issues*, Vol. 2, pp. 267–73. Chichester: Wiley.

Howe, M. J. A. (1988b) Intelligence as an explanation. *British Journal of Psychology*, **79**: 349–60.

Howe, M. J. A. (1988c) The hazards of using correlational evidence as a means of identifying the causes of individual ability differences: a rejoinder to Sternberg and a reply to Miles. *British Journal of Psychology*, **79**: 539–45.

Howe, M. J. A. (1988d) Context, memory and education. In Davies, G. M. and Thomson, D. M. (eds), *Memory in Context: Context in Memory*, pp. 267–81. Chichester: Wiley.

Howe, M. J. A. (1988e) 'Hot house' children. *The Psychologist*, **1**: 356–8.

Howe, M. J. A. (1988f) Perspiration beats inspiration. *New Scientist*, **120** (1644/1645): 58–60.

Howe, M. J. A. (1989a) *Fragments of Genius: the Strange Feats of Idiots Savants*. London: Routledge.

Howe, M. J. A. (1989b) 'Idiots savants'. In Eysenck, M. W., Ellis, A., Hunt, E. and Johnson-Laird, P. (eds), *Dictionary of Cognitive Psychology*. Oxford: Blackwell.

Howe, M. J. A. (1989c) The hot house effect. *Child Education*, **66**(3): 20–1.

Howe, M. J. A. (1990a) (ed.): *Encouraging the Development of Exceptional Abilities and Talents*. Leicester: The British Psychological Society.

Howe, M. J. A. (1990b) *Sense and Nonsense about Hothouse Children: A Practical Guide for Parents and Teachers*. London: The British Psychological Society.

Howe, M. J. A. (1997) *IQ in Question: The Truth About Intelligence*. London: Sage.

Howe, M. J. A. (1998) Early lives: prodigies and non-prodigies. In Steptoe, A. (ed.): *Genius and the Mind*. Oxford: Oxford University Press.

Howe, M. J. A., Davidson, J. W., Moore, G. and Sloboda, J. A. (1995) Are there early signs of musical ability? *Psychology of Music*, **23**: 162–176.

Howe, M. J. A., Davidson, J. W. and Sloboda, J. A. (1998) Innate Talents: Reality or Myth? *Behavioral and Brain Sciences*, **21**: 399–442.

Hunt, J. McV. (1986) The effect of variations in quality and type of early child care on development. In Fowler, W. (ed.), *Early Experience and the Development of Competence: No. 32, New Directions for Child Development*. San Francisco: Jossey-Bass.

Jersild, A. T. and Bienstock, S. F. (1931) The influence of training on the vocal ability of three-year-old children. *Child Development*, **2**: 272–91.

Kamin, L. (1995) Lies, damned lies, and statistics. In Jacoby, R. and Gauberman, N. (eds), *The Bell Curve Debate*. New York: Times Books.

Keating, D. P. (1976) Creative potential of mathematically precocious boys. In Keating, D. P. (ed.), *Intellectual Talent: Research and Development. Proceedings of the Sixth Annual Hyman Blumberg Symposium on Research in Early Childhood Education*. Baltimore: Johns Hopkins University Press.

Keating, D. P. (1984) The emperor's new clothes: The 'new look' in intelligence research. In Sternberg, R. J. (ed.), *Advances in the Psychology of Human Intelligence*, Vol. 2. Hillsdale, New Jersey: Erlbaum.

Klemp, G. O. and McClelland, D. C. (1986) What characterizes intelligent functioning among senior managers? In Sternberg, R. J. and Wagner, R. K. (eds), *Practical Intelligence: Nature and Origins of*

Competence in the Everyday World. Cambridge: Cambridge University Press.

Kress, G. (1982) *Learning to Write*. London: Routledge.

Lave, J. (1988) *Cognition in Practice: Mind, Mathematics and Culture in Everyday Life*. New York: Cambridge University Press.

Lazar, L., Darlington, R., Murray, H., Royce, J. and Snippet, A. (1982) Lasting effects of early education: a report from the Consortium for Longitudinal Studies. *Monographs of the Society for Research in Child Development*, **47**: 2–3. (Serial No. 195).

Lehman, H. C. (1953) *Age and Achievement*. Princetown, New Jersey: Princetown University Press.

Lennon, P. (1989) Sweeping the board by book or by rook. *Guardian*, 11 November.

Lewontin, R. (1982) *Human Diversity*. New York: Freeman.

Lowes, J. L. (1927) *The Road to Xanadu*. Boston: Houghton Mifflin.

Luria, A. R. (1968) *The Mind of a Mnemonist*. New York: Basic Books.

McCartney, K. (1984) Effects of quality of day care environment on children's language development. *Developmental Psychology*, **20**: 244–60.

McClelland, D. C. (1973) Testing for competence rather than for 'intelligence'. *American Psychologist*, **28**: 1–14.

McGraw, M. (1935) *Growth: A Study of Johnny and Jimmy*. New York: Appleton-Century-Crofts.

McGraw, M. (1939) Later development of children specially trained during infancy: Johnny and Jimmy at school age. *Child Development*, **10**: 1–19.

MacKenzie, N. and MacKenzie, J. (1973) *The Life of H. G. Wells: The Time Traveller*. London: Weidenfeld & Nicholson.

Marjoram, D. T. E. and Nelson, R. D. (1985) Mathematical gifts. In Freeman, J. (ed.), *The Psychology of Gifted Children*. Chichester: Wiley.

Mead, M. (1975) *Growing up in New Guinea*. New York: William Morrow.

Metzl, M. N. (1980) Teaching parents a strategy for enhancing infant development. *Child Development*, **51**: 583–6.

Mill, J. S. (1971) *Autobiography*. London: Oxford University Press. (First published in 1873.)

Moon, C. and Wells, G. (1979) The influence of home on learning to read. *Journal of Research in Reading*, **2**: 53–62.

Morris, P. E. (1988) Expertise and everyday memory. In Gruneberg, M. M., Morris, P. E. and Sykes, R. N. (eds), *Practical Aspects of Memory: Current Research and Issues*, Vol. 1. Chichester: Wiley.

Morris, P. E., Gruneberg, M. M., Sykes, R. N. and Merrick, A. (1981) Football knowledge and the acquisition of new results. *British Journal of Psychology*, **72**: 479–83.

Morris, P. E., Tweedy, M. and Gruneberg, M. M. (1985) Interest, knowledge and the memorizing of soccer scores. *British Journal of Psychology*, **76**: 415–25.

Nelson, K. (1977) Facilitating children's syntax acquisition. *Developmental Psychology*, **13**: 101–7.

Nelson, K., Carskaddon, G. and Bonvillian, J. D. (1973) Syntax acquisition: impact of experimental variation in adult verbal interaction with the child. *Child Development*, **44**: 497–504.

Olson, D. R. (1977) From utterance to text: the basis of language in speech and writing. *Harvard Educational Review*, **47**: 257–82.

Olson, D. R. (1986) Intelligence and literacy: the relationships between intelligence and the technologies of representation and communication. In Sternberg, R. J. and Wagner, R. K. (eds), *Practical Intelligence: Nature and Origins of Competence in the Everyday World*, pp. 338–60. Cambridge: Cambridge University Press.

Ong, W. J. (1982) *Orality and Literacy: the Technologizing of the Word*. London: Methuen.

Patel, V. L., Kaufman, D. R. and Magder, S. A. (1996) The acquisition of medical expertise in complex dynamic environments. In Ericsson, K. A. (ed.), *The Road to Excellence; The Acquisiton of Expert Performance in the Arts and Sciences, Sports and Games*. Mahwah, New Jersey: Erlbaum.

Peak, L. (1986) Training learning skills and attitudes in Japanese early educational settings. In Fowler, W. (ed.), *Early Experience and the Development of Competence. No. 32. New Directions for Child Development*. San Francisco: Jossey-Bass.

Perkins, D. N. (1981) *The Mind's Best Work*. London: Harvard University Press.

Petersen, G. A. and Sherrod, K. B. (1982) Relationship of maternal language to language development and language delay of children. *American Journal of Mental Deficiency*, **86**: 391–8.

Pinker, S. (1994) *The Language Instinct*. London: Penguin.

Pinker, S. (1997) *How the Mind Works*. London: Penguin.

Radford, J. (1990) *Child Prodigies and Exceptional Early Achievement*. London: Harvester.

Ramey, C. T., Bryant, D. M. and Suarez, T. (1985) Preschool compensatory education and the modifiability of intelligence: a critical review. In Detterman, D. K. (ed.), *Current Topics in Human Intelligence*. Norwood, New Jersey: Ablex.

Renzulli, J. S. (1986) The three-ring conception of giftedness: a developmental model for creative productivity. In Sternberg, R. J. and Davidson, J. E. (eds), *Conceptions of Giftedness*. New York: Cambridge University Press.

Roe, A. (1952) *The Making of a Scientist*. New York: Dodd, Mead.

Rolfe, L. M. (1978) *The Menuhins: a Family Odyssey*. San Francisco: Panjandrum / Aris Books.

Rothenberg, A. (1979) *The Emerging Goddess: The Creative Process in Art, Science, and Other Fields*. Chicago: University of Chicago Press.

Rutter, M. (1989) Pathways from childhood to adult life. *Journal of Child Psychology and Psychiatry*, **30**: 23–51.

Saxe, G. B. (1988) The mathematics of child street vendors. *Child Development*, **59**: 1415–25.

Schlaug, G., Jänke, L., Huang, Y. and Steinmetz, H. (1995) *In vivo* evidence of structural brain asymetry in musicians. *Science*, **267**: 699–701.

Scribner, S. (1986) Thinking in action: some characteristics of practical thought. In Sternberg, R. J. and Wagner, R. K. (eds), *Practical Intelligence: Nature and Origins of Competence in the Everyday World*. Cambridge: Cambridge University Press.

Shuter-Dyson, R. and Gabriel, C. (1981) *The Psychology of Musical Ability*, 2nd edn. London: Methuen.

Simon, H. A. and Chase, W. G. (1973) Skill in chess. *American Scientist*, **61**: 394–403.

Skidelsky, R. (1983) *John Maynard Keynes*. Vol. 1. *Hopes Betrayed*. London: Macmillan.

Sloane, K. D. (1985) Home influences on talent development. In Bloom, B. S. (ed.), *Developing Talent in Young People*. New York: Ballantine.

Sloboda, J. A. (1985) *The Musical Mind: the Cognitive Psychology of Music*. London: Oxford University Press.

Sloboda, J. A. and Howe, M. J. A. (1991) Biographical precursors of musical excellence: an interview study. *Psychology of Music*, **19**: 3–21.

Sloboda, J. A., Davidson, J. W., Howe, M. J. A. and Moore, D. G. (1996) The role of practice in the development of performing musicians. *British Journal of Psychology*, **87**: 287–309.

Smith, S. B. (1983) *The Great Mental Calculators*. New York: Columbia University Press.

Sorokin, P. (1956) *Fads and Foibles in Modern Sociology*, Chicago: H. Regnery.

Sosniak, L. A. (1985) Learning to be a concert pianist. In Bloom, B. S. (ed.), *Developing Talent in Young People*. New York: Ballantine.

Sosniak, L. A. (1990) The tortoise, the hare, and the development of talent. In Howe, M. J. A. (ed.), *Encouraging the Development of Exceptional Abilities and Talents*. Leicester: The British Psychological Society.

Staats, A. W. (1971) *Child Learning, Intelligence, and Personality*. New York: Harper & Row.

Stanley, J. C., George, W. C. and Solano, C. H. (1977) *The Gifted and the Creative*. Baltimore: Johns Hopkins University Press.

Starkes, J. L., Deakin, J. M., Allard, F., Hodges, N. J. and Hayes, A. (1996) Deliberate practice in sports: what is it anyway? In Ericsson, K.A. (ed.), *The Road to Excellence; The Acquisiton of Expert Performance in the Arts and Sciences, Sports and Games*. Mahwah, New Jersey: Erlbaum.

Stott, D.H. (1974) *The Parent as Teacher: A Guide for Parents of Children with Learning Difficulties*. London: University of London Press.

Super, C. (1976) Environmental effects on motor development: the case of 'African infant precocity'. *Developmental Medicine and Child Neurology*, **18**: 561–7.

Taniuchi, L. (1986) Cultural continuity in an educational institution: a case study of the Suzuki method of music instruction. In White, M. I. and Pollak, S. (eds), *The Cultural Transition: Human Experience and Social Transformation in the Third World and Japan*. Boston: Routledge and Kegan Paul.

Valdez-Menchaca, M. C. and Whitehurst, G. J. (1988) The effects of incidental teaching on vocabulary acquisition by young children. *Child Development*, **59**: 1451–9.

Wachs, T. D. and Gruen, G. E. (1982) *Early Experience and Human Development*. New York: Plenum Press.

Wallace, A. (1986) *The Prodigy: A Biography of William James Sidis, the World's Greatest Child Prodigy*. London: Macmillan.

Weinert, F. E. and Waldmann, M. R. (1986) How do the gifted think?: intellectual abilities and cognitive processes. In Cropley, A. J., Urban, K. K., Wagner, H. and Wieczerkowski, W. (eds), *Giftedness: a Continuing Worldwide Challenge*. New York: Trillium Press.

Weisberg, R. (1986) *Creativity: Genius and Other Myths*. New York: Freeman.

Weisberg, R. W. (1993) *Creativity: Beyond the Myth of Genius*. New York: Freeman.

Westfall, R. S. (1980) Newton's marvellous years of discovery and their aftermath: myth versus manuscript. *Isis*, **71**(256): 109–21.

White, B. L. (1985) Competence and giftedness. In Freeman, J. (ed.), *The Psychology of Gifted Children*. Chichester: Wiley.

Whitehurst, G. J. and Valdez-Menchaca, M. C. (1988) What is the role of reinforcement in early language acquisition? *Child Development*, **59**: 430–40.

Whitehurst, G. J., Falco, F. L., Lonigan, C. J., Fischel, J. E., DeBaryshe, B. D., Valdez-Menchaca, M. C. and Caulfield, M. (1988) Accelerating language development through picture book reading. *Developmental Psychology*, **24**: 552–9.

Wiener, N. (1953) *Ex-Prodigy: My Childhood and Youth*. New York: Simon & Schuster.

Winner, E. (1996) *Gifted Children: Myths and Realities*. New York: Basic Books.

Witte, K. H. G. (1975) *The Education of Karl Witte*, trans. Leo Wiener. New York: Arno Press. (English translation originally published in 1914 by Thomas Cromwell.)

Zigler, E. and Seitz, V. (1982) Social policy and intelligence. In Sternberg, R. J. (ed.), *Handbook of Human Intelligence*. New York: Cambridge University Press.

Zuckerman, H. (1977) *Scientific Elite: Nobel Laureates in the United States*. New York: Free Press.

Index